Fur Trapping in North America

Fur Trapping in North America
Revised Edition

Steven M. Geary

WINCHESTER PRESS
An Imprint of New Century Publishers, Inc.

Dedication:
This one's just for Jacquie

Acknowledgments:
The author would like to thank Kathy Robinson, for special help in creating line art, and Russ Reagan, for extraordinary assistance in photography.

Fur Trapping in North America © 1984, 1981
by Steven M. Geary

Revised Edition
Manufactured in the United States of America

Printing Code
11 12 13 14 15 16

Library of Congress Cataloging in Publication Data
Geary, Steven M.
   Fur trapping in North America.

   Includes index.
   1. Trapping—North America. 2. Wildlife conservation
—North America. I. Title.
SK283.6.N7G43   1984   639'.11'097   84-16561
ISBN 0-8329-0367-1
ISBN 0-8329-0368-X (pbk.)

Contents

1 The Role of Trapping Today   1
2 Preparation   5
3 The Equipment   22
4 The Animals   63
5 Basic Sets   109
6 Handling the Catch from Trap to Market   123
7 A Few Final Words – Ethics   147
Appendix: Trapping Suppliers and Organizations   149
Index   153

1 THE ROLE OF TRAPPING TODAY

Trapping plays a role – a very important role – in the conservation of natural resources as we pass through the waning years of the 20th century. The fact is that nothing else promotes the highest and best use of the furbearer resource as does the individual trapper with his handful of steel traps or snares. And there is a lot to be said for good management of the resource.

The main product of the harvest of surplus furbearers, of course, is fur clothing. Since only the surplus animals are taken, the furbearers are excellent examples of a renewable resource; with careful management, the resource should last forever, and a great decline in the harvest or population in general would almost certainly result from habitat destruction rather than trapping pressure. Ecologically speaking, fur clothing is relatively inexpensive in terms of energy expended from nonrenewable sources – such as fossil fuels in production of other clothing. Synthetics used in clothing are relatively costly, whether they come from nonrenewable fossil fuels such as coal or oil or from energy-intensive resources such as cellulose or wood fiber.

There is another side to the cost-saving view of furbearers. These animals can be very destructive if their numbers are not controlled. Peak populations of muskrat and beaver can be destructive to fruit trees and other forestry resources. Losses from muskrat-riddled pond dams and irrigation walls are estimated to run into millions of dollars annually. Weasel, coyote, and fox ravage domestic fowl in addition to wild prey when these furbearers' numbers get too high. Despite record high prices for wool and lamb, several states have had declines in sheep ranching as a result of great losses sustained from predation. Western states have reported predator losses of sheep valued in the millions in recent years. Failure to harvest excess furbearers can result not only in wasted pelts, but in domestic animal loss and other damages, sometimes to the land itself.

Despite all this, trapping has long been a highly controversial subject. One scoffing criticism is that harvests of wild fur could not begin to approach the human needs for warm clothing. This, of course, overlooks the obvious: The fur harvest frees a proportionate amount of resources that otherwise would have gone into clothing production. More important, furbearers that exist in harvestable numbers are a resource that cannot be stockpiled. Any piece of wildlife habitat is said to have a finite "carrying capacity" – meaning that the land can support only a certain number of animals – and the furbearers in excess of the carrying capacity will invariably fall prey to disease, starvation, or simple exposure. The cycle is always the same. Perhaps the most dramatic example of damage to both habitat and the furbearer itself that periodically results from overpopulation is the so-called "eat-out" by muskrats. When muskrat populations peak, the animals routinely denude their entire habitat, which results in a long-term decline in habitat *for other animals as well as the muskrats*. Animals lost to disease, starvation, predation, and other causes are wasted or at least lost for human use. It is simply poor management of the resource to support total protection when the resource is so cyclical and incapable of being stockpiled. The key is conservation – wise use rather than hopeless efforts at preservation.

Beaver dam (photo by Mark Brown)

The most commonly raised objection to trapping, however, is the emotional charge of cruelty. When the entire list of criticisms is carefully reviewed, this well intentioned – if poorly reasoned – sentiment is all the anti-trappers have to say.

The accusation of cruelty is not well founded. Organizations dedicated to the abolition of trapping sometimes display some hideous, jagged-toothed trap as evidence of the inhumanity of trapping. The fact is such relics are outdated curiosities which never had much use and which, in any event, have been illegal for decades. Other evidence of supposedly widespread cruelty is the occasional horror scene of a maimed or otherwise suffering furbearer struggling pitifully or dangling from a poorly constructed snare. These scenes are not at all typical. At worst, they are the work of the tiny percentage of trappers who are careless and irresponsible. No trapper takes pleasure in the pain or suffering of furbearers. On the contrary, trappers make every effort to keep the time spent by animals in the trap at a minimum and the actual killing as humane as possible.

All trappers – and trappers' suppliers and associations – have made every effort to design humane traps. New, humane snares have recently been perfected and are now on the market. They may revolutionize the sport. The conibear, or body-gripping trap, is another example of a humane trap that captures the animal and kills it quickly with very little suffering. A conibear has an obvious limiting factor, however, in that an occasional nontarget animal may wander into it. The use of the conibear is therefore limited to small sizes or sets where domestic animals are not present, such as in water or in very high places. The live trap also has its place, as the captured animal experiences no suffering with the possible exception of some degree of exposure. Live traps, unfortunately, are very bulky and for that reason are unsuitable for use in large numbers or in remote places.

Since the use of killer-type traps and live traps has been thus more or less restricted, the only method that remains for an efficient harvest of the fur resource is the steel leghold trap. This trap has become the number one target of those who would ban trapping. The horror stories about such traps are either mostly nonsense or the result of outrageous, illegal behavior. The suffering of animals in leghold traps has been greatly exaggerated, since the clamping effect of a properly matched trap does very little damage. The author has personally released, uninjured, a nontarget squirrel and even a mouse from leghold traps. The clamping effect of the trap quickly results in numbness, and the trap and drag merely restrict the animal's movements. A properly constructed drowning set dispatches the animal very quickly. Dry-land sets that use the leghold trap cause no great suffering either. An accompanying photograph shows a trapped fox which is not suffering at all; the author has witnessed such animals actually sleeping in leghold traps. As an example of the lengths to which trappers and manufacturers of trapping equipment have gone to make leghold traps as painless as possible, there is now available a trap with the jaws offset. The jaws do not match perfectly and this results in less pressure on the leg or foot. The only obvious limiting factor is that the trap must hold fast enough to prevent escape.

The problem then is overcoming the emotionalism attached to what the onlooker might perceive as suffering of the furbearers. The tendency to give human characteristics to animals — variously called the Bambi syndrome or anthropomorphism — rarely vanishes in the face of logic. But it should be remembered that wild animals very rarely die painlessly or peacefully. Falling prey to a trapper is no more brutal an ordeal than any other death in the wild, where nature is neither kind nor cruel but simply indifferent.

Trapping, then, is the one effective management tool for the wild fur resource, just as surely as the ax is a management tool for our timber resource. Through the intelligent use of the resource, we approach a maximum sustained yield without damage to any species of animal. Without this management tool, the resource is wasted.

Red fox held by steel leghold trap.

2 Preparation

SCOUTING

A trapper who lays out a trapline without scouting might as well travel to a foreign country not knowing the language, carrying a map, or hiring a guide. In large tracts of what is normally termed furbearer habitat, only a few key places will contain the vast majority of furbearers. By the estimate of many widely experienced trappers, ninety percent of all the animals are located in two percent of all the trapping territory. Scouting enables the trapper to make his sets in that productive two percent.

Trapping seasons are traditionally very short and ordinarily are accompanied by unsettled weather with vast ranges of temperatures and widely fluctuating water conditions, which further reduce the number of days that may be used for trapping. Therefore, precious are the first few days of the season, which are usually the mildest and, accordingly, free of ice which might stymie the water set trapper. During this time, most animals are active and not yet trap shy. To spend several days of the short season adjusting the trapline to maximum efficiency is simply untenable. Besides, preseason scouting is an opportunity to mill through the trapping grounds and enjoy other pursuits—fishing, berry picking, or simple hiking — while narrowing the area to a trapline. This is important to remember: a trapper does not trap an entire area; he chooses an area and traps a single line through it. The line must be well chosen for maximum success.

Terrain

Places to trap are not necessarily found in remote, untrammeled country. Many good, although small, trap grounds are found adjacent to civilization or within city limits. Skeptics about the suburban trapline would do well to review local conservation department statistics which break out the fur harvest county by county. From 1977 to 1978, the most populous Missouri counties of Jackson, which contains Kansas City and St. Louis, yielded 926 opossums, 38 skunks, 1,699 muskrats, 2,809 raccoons, 62 mink, 232 coyote, and 67 beaver. Not a bad harvest for the few trappers who know how to scout out the fur available close to a metropolitan area. Once a territory is located that appears wild enough to contain furbearers, scouting for the best spots can begin.

Initially, the trapper will be looking primarily for furbearer shelter. Small caves or crevices in a bluff are worth a second look. Holes dug in dirt or sandy spots may harbor furbearers and may be places to consider as sites for dirt-hole sets. Large deadfalls or, even better, piles of trees cleared from farmland can be excellent places for skunk, opossum, or raccoon to den up. Extremely large trees should be scouted for holes which may be dens for opossum or raccoon; the large, exposed roots of such trees may be dens as well and, if not, may be natural cubbies during the season.

Field edges or borders where several types of cover exist are also likely spots. Clearing rubble that sits on the edge of a field grown up in goldenrod, ragweed, or elderberries is a good site. Such an area is surrounded by numerous productive trapping spots for all furbearers other than those associated with water. Thick stands of elderberries, chokecherries, or persimmons are good possibilities. Dense cover with adjacent cornfields can provide exceptionally good spots for finding raccoon. The very dense cover offered by wild blackberry brambles is a good place to look for raccoon, opossum, and weasel.

Water is, of course, an essential element for trapping muskrats and beaver; it may present good prospects for mink and raccoon as well. Probably the best water sources for trapping these furbearers are ponds and slow-running streams with dirt banks and a wide variety of cover. Muskrats tend to gather to feed where there are dense stands of willow saplings or reeds. Beaver dams are unmistakable and are obviously good places for sets. The overhanging banksides of small streams are good places for muskrat and mink sets. In fact, small tributaries or branches are such likely prospects for mink that they have been termed "mink streams" by old-timers. Scouting should detect den holes in banks of ponds and streams.

Trapper examining a mink stream. (courtesy J.E. Osman and
the Pennsylvania Game Commission)

Large, exposed roots are common near water and may be dens. If
not, they can still serve as natural cubbies and productive locations for
sets, whether or not baited, for mink, raccoon, and muskrat.

Sloping logs that lie partially in water can be ideal sites for water
sets. Logs which are entirely on dry ground also can be productive, but
will require other techniques to be successful.

In brief, any place where furbearers might concentrate their activity
or travel is a good choice. This concentration could result from a food
preference or from an obstruction, whether natural or man-made, such
as a bridge or road.

Sign

In addition to good terrain, the preseason trapper will be scouting
for sign, the visible evidence that the animals sought are in the area. The
trapper must now become a student of nature and survey the area with
great care. The sign left by furbearers is ordinarily very subtle: a few
scratches, tracks, scats, or a bit of hair in a tight spot.

The most obvious and most reliable sign are the tracks of the animals desired. Trappers look for tracks in mud flats or, in season, a powdering of snow. The tracks of the various animals can seem very similar to the novice. The accompanying illustrations may assist in identifying the different tracks.

Scats and tracks of various furbearers.

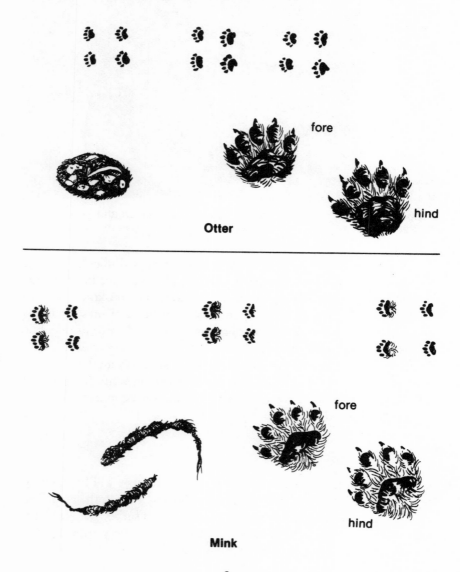

fore

hind

Otter

fore

hind

Mink

8

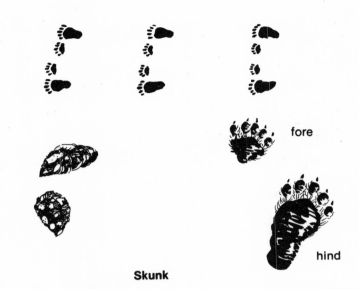

fore

hind

Skunk

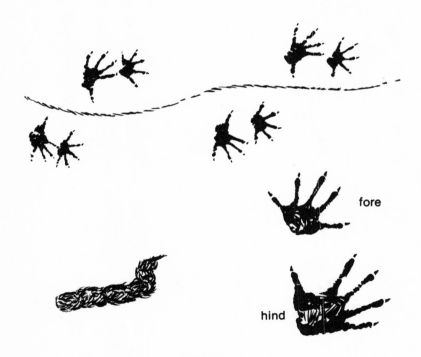

fore

hind

Opossum

9

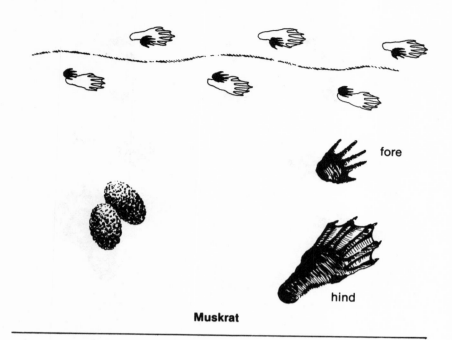

Muskrat

fore

hind

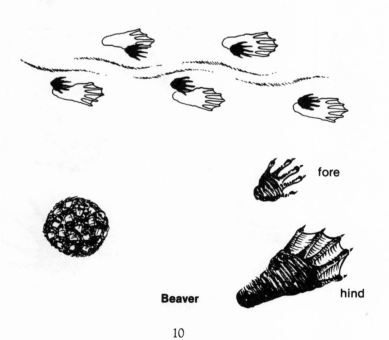

Beaver

fore

hind

10

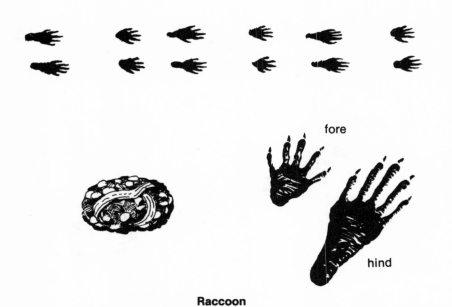

Raccoon

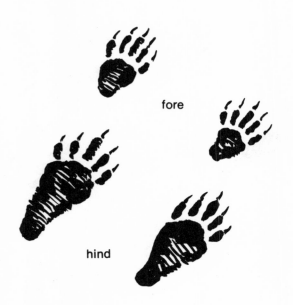

Badger

11

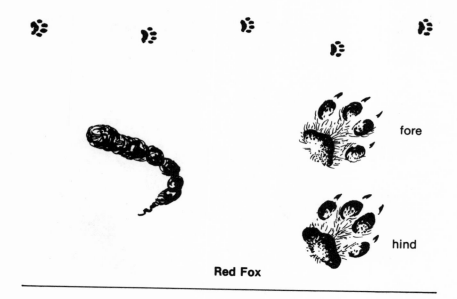

Red Fox

fore

hind

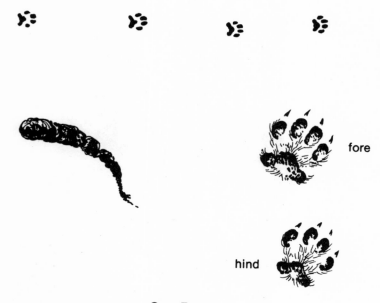

fore

hind

Gray Fox

12

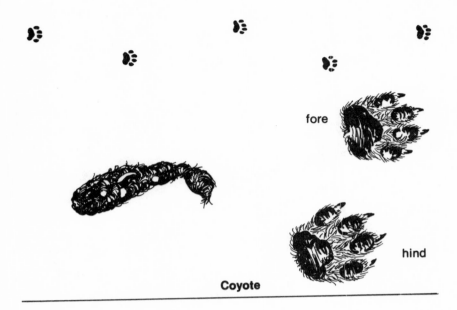

Coyote

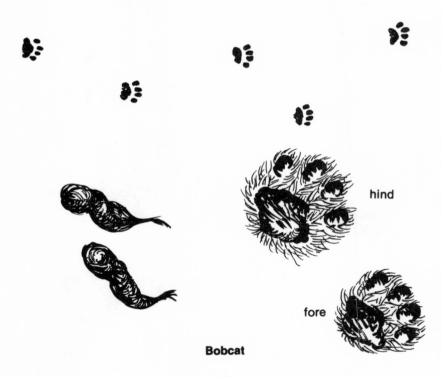

Bobcat

13

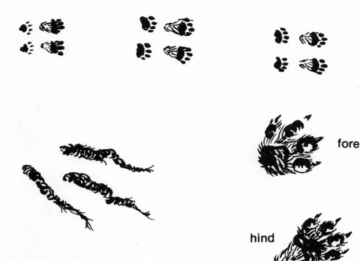

fore

hind

Weasel

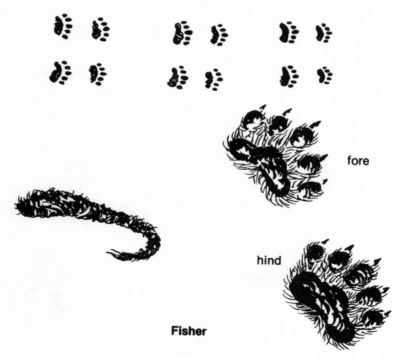

fore

hind

Fisher

14

Droppings or scats are also reliable sign. The concentration of the droppings often serves as a clue to the location of the feeding grounds and the type of food currently favored by the furbearers. The size and shape of the scats can tell a skilled observer what furbearers have passed by and when. Again, all scats will seem the same to the beginner, but perhaps the accompanying illustrations will make identification easier.

Beaver and muskrat often leave convenient, unmistakable signs in the form of teeth marks — beaver on larger trees and muskrat on saplings. Muskrat also commonly leave a slurry of weed cuttings in the water where they have been feeding; the slurried water looks churned up and cloudy with bits of twigs and leaves floating in it.

Beaver and muskrat also leave very obvious evidence of their whereabouts in the highly visible houses they build. Beaver houses are distinctive in appearance because they are very sizable and made of relatively large logs and earth. Channels, or other signs indicating entry and exit points around the house, should be in evidence and will make excellent places for sets. Muskrat houses are similar in design but are much smaller and more numerous.

Runs, by definition, include sets of tracks, but even without clear footprints some runs can be spotted and will make first-rate sites for killer-type sets. Runs tend to follow large obstructions or edges of cover. For example, large fallen trees often serve to define the line of a run, as do fences and large buildings or natural outcroppings. The depopulation of rural regions has left numerous small farmsteads abandoned. The overgrown old farms and tangled areas around the forsaken buildings can be fairly riddled with furbearer runs.

Channels are the underwater equivalent of runs. Most commonly associated with muskrats, the channel also can be located near beaver or otter habitat. Channels are paths that semiaquatic furbearers follow regularly because of convenience to food or exceptionally good protection from some natural enemy. They are easily spotted in very shallow, clear water as a gentle depression slightly darker than the rest of the bottom. As with runs, these channels can be excellent places for sets, especially when some other natural condition such as an overhanging bank makes passing through a specific, confined area very attractive.

Notes

Trappers who spend any time at all scouting for proper terrain and signs will do well to take some notes about the findings. It is easy to delude oneself into thinking that memory will serve, but even the best memory is fallible and errors of a few feet can be critical in trapping. In addition, most trappers will be covering so much territory in scouting that notes are essential for recalling the number of sets to be used in an area and to describe a plan of attack in laying out a trapline. Even the part-time trapper with plans for a very small line may set lines in such a way as to require successive trips by car or may use one trapline early in the season and others later.

Brief notes, in the trapper's own shorthand if desired, are best. For example, an especially attractive site for a muskrat or mink set consisting of a huge tree with roots exposed and partially in water might be noted as follows: oak, wet/dry, mink-rat, 100 yds S of Beaver Dam Westbank.

EARLY PREPARATION — IN THE FIELD

Preseason scouting of an area is really just the first half of a thorough preparation for trapping. When looking for sign in likely habitat, the trapper cannot help thinking about prime places for sets; the trained eye drifts toward exposed roots, rock crevices, and natural outcroppings. The next step is to fashion the artificial spots that will be needed to supplement the natural trap sites. Preseason work makes sense and will pay off in precious time saved early in the season when furbearers are most numerous and a trapper is not hobbled by frozen water sets, snow, and other problems associated with bitter cold. During the preparation stages, a trapper is really laying out the trapline. It is wise to lay out the line in a manner that eliminates covering any territory twice on a single trip, both to save time and to reduce the possibility of leaving alerting human signs. In addition, the trapper should think in terms of trapping all species available. While skunk, opossum, and weasel do not bring nearly the price of raccoon or mink, setting traps for the more common animals is a good idea, especially when the sets can be made without covering extra territory. The gaps between mink or fox traps must be covered in any case. Good planning will dot those spaces with traps for the more common animals and will maximize the yield.

Cubbies

Furbearers are attracted to baited or unbaited cubbies which are nothing more than enclosures with one open side with a trap strategically placed. Apparently, the cubby arouses the curiosity of the passing furbearer; the unbaited sets could never be so successful based on the law of random chance alone. The curious animal enters by the only route available and passes over the trap. Generally speaking, cubbies can be readily made, most often of natural materials found on sight. Properly constructed cubbies may last for several seasons.

Small cubbies for mink or weasel can be made easily from scrap lumber: a top, two sides, and a back with no bottom and an open front. Put in place days or weeks in advance, the cubby quickly will become a part of the natural surroundings as leaves and twigs settle around it.

A dozen or so stove-length logs piled together tepee style, or similar to a thatched hut or pup tent closed at one end, will make an attractive cubby for larger furbearers such as raccoon and possum. Some trappers prefer to use a chain saw and make the cubby in the preseason.

Some cubbies are made by incorporating natural crevices and outcroppings. A large stone with a crevice, or two large stones together, can be made into a cubby for raccoon, possum, or skunk by closing one end and covering the top with natural materials, such as sticks and bark. A large fallen tree trunk with a well-positioned branch might serve as one side and back of a cubby, needing only to be closed with sticks to attract weasel, marten, fisher, raccoon, possum, or skunk.

If left undisturbed long enough, entirely artificial apparatus can be used for cubbies. Trappers occasionally use five-gallon paint or tar cans, turned on one side, as cubbies with good success. Likewise, medium-sized cardboard boxes work as long as weather remains clear and mild.

Holes

Holes for dirt-hole sets and bait-hole sets are best dug prior to the season. The dirt hole is the rough equivalent of an unbaited cubby and a baited hole coincides with a baited cubby. The hole is located in an area of great furbearer activity and a trap is placed at the mouth where a curious animal is likely to tread. There are two obvious reasons for digging the holes early. First, the time factor is very much on the trapper's side. Not only is more time available to get holes dug where they belong, but digging will be much easier without frozen ground and muck to contend with prior to the opening of the season. Second, the hole dug early will become more natural looking either from the elements or from water slopped into the hole to smooth out the spade marks. A trapper should remember the wide fluctuation of water conditions when making the holes; where the water tends to rise and fall, several extra holes at varying depths are advisable.

Floaters

Muskrat trappers — and that includes a remarkably high percentage of *all* trappers — can serve themselves well by employing a floating-log set or several such sets. Floaters, two medium logs or a single large log notched to hold traps and with holes bored for bait sticks, take time to make. However, they are extremely productive — often over an entire season. Once a colony of muskrats is located and the log is placed, the trapper needs only to set the steel. A good nylon cord staked out to hold the floating set will permit the set to adjust itself to whatever water conditions develop. Plans to finish this work on the floating-log set should anticipate two hours to do the job properly. This, of course, should be done in advance of the season. Perhaps a better and quicker way is to use a large plank with cleats and several traps, rather than a log. In any event, this type of set should be made in advance of the actual season.

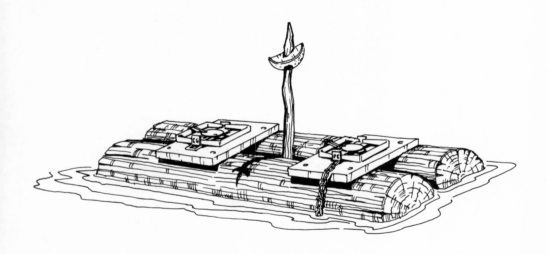

Floating log set

18

Baiting

Preseason baiting can be an effective way of concentrating furbearers around the traps — a bit of indirect production as the economists would term it. However, this form of preseason preparation may be illegal in some jurisdictions. Local codes should be studied before baiting is undertaken.

Baiting an area will work for most furbearers. Some furbearers — most notably muskrats — are not really roamers in the ordinary sense. They follow more or less predictable patterns that can be detected from tracks or channels on the bottom of the body of water they occupy. They are not too likely to be drawn long distances to take bait, preseason or not. However, a little bait on a floating log set prior to the season or scattered in a selected spot which would be especially convenient for several sets can get the muskrats making the rounds to where the bait is during the preseason and where both bait and traps will be later.

Most furbearers roam considerable distances overland and preseason baiting can serve to concentrate the animals where the traps are to be set. An occasional bit of tainted meat in a hollow log or rock overhang will get fox, coyote, and skunk interested and visiting regularly. A gob bait or head from a chicken or goose attached to a tree high enough to make a raccoon or possum reach and stretch for it will make the scene well visited and a good spot for a couple of traps to be baited during the season, with a similar attraction.

Dirt-hole sets and cubbies can be assured of regular visitors who will thoroughly investigate the site if a few minnows or fish entrails are tossed in to bring the furbearers around.

A commonly overlooked aspect of baiting, whether preseason or in-season, is general broadcasting of bait materials. Baiting is, after all, designed to bring the animals within the range of the trap. If this means bringing them close and then precisely to the pan, broadcasting can be a good idea. Small bits of fragrant cooked turkey skins or lard cracklings sown like chicken feed will make an area interesting to all carnivorous and scavenging furbearers. Deer hair shaved from a hide and scattered near proposed sets will attract the same range of animals. Likewise, a scattering of small bits of chicken bones or feathers can produce the same effect. Cut fruit such as watermelon, rind and all, or whole persimmons will attract raccoon, skunk, and possum.

A final word...casting about for furbearers prior to the season can be very worthwhile. In addition to the obvious improvements that can be made by building cubbies and noting likely spots, more subtle changes can make the preseason efforts valuable. Note tracks and feed beds, but also take the time to narrow trails with rocks or logs. Make a little map for later, but move a few hollowed-out logs to streamside for mink to travel through. In brief, think in terms of making the trapline the best possible place before the season begins.

A FEW WORDS ABOUT THE LAW

Actually, the expression "the law" is misleading. Because there are so many jurisdictions with their own trapping laws, it is virtually impossible to generalize concerning what "the law" is.

Within the United States there are dozens of jurisdictions, each of which has its own conservation commission or department of natural resources or both. Each commission or department, responding to the various attitudes, pressures, and conditions within its jurisdiction, generates law which is peculiar to its needs. For example, some jurisdictions — generally those in the Southwestern United States — consider the bobcat a varmint and it therefore is, or has been, totally unprotected. Other jurisdictions are concerned that the bobcat is threatened with extinction primarily through lost habitat, but also to a limited extent as a result of hunting or trapping pressure. These jurisdictions have responded by closing the season altogether. Still others have felt it appropriate to steer a crooked course in monitoring the bobcat population and have had an open but controlled season followed by complete protection, only to reopen on a very restricted basis.

Season lengths are another matter where wide variations are the rule. Some states treat certain furbearers as varmints by foregoing any protection, either for hunting or trapping, such as that described above for the bobcat in certain areas or for the raccoon in others. Some jurisdictions permit hunting of certain animals year-round but trapping only at specified times. The opening and closing dates of the hunting and trapping seasons vary widely, also. Some jurisdictions vary the season species by species as justified by fluctuating animal populations. Missouri, for example, has extended beaver trapping weeks beyond the end of the rest of the trapping season because the animal's population permits and, in fact necessitates use of this method of control.

Equipment limitations vary among jurisdictions and even from season to season within given jurisdictions. For example, Missouri has used what some have called a "succession to extinction" approach to the killer trap, successively reducing the maximum size permitted on land sets to the point that many trappers find the conibear an unacceptable choice. Numerous states prohibit the use of snares and deadfalls. Others permit, prohibit, or restrict the use of the humane trap.

The lesson of all of this is clear: No trapper should begin a season without a thorough review of the current laws in his jurisdictions. This review is necessary every season, in all locations, as the laws continue to evolve.

3 The Equipment

TRAPS

Deadfalls

No trapping commentary would be complete, it seems, without at least passing mention of the more primitive trapping devices known as deadfalls. Deadfalls are outlawed in most jurisdictions and are not in common use as most trappers feel they are simply too brutal to be employed; no trappers' association in the world has anything good to say about deadfalls because of the obvious public relations problems associated with these sets. The deadfall, as the name implies, is any one of several types of trapping devices that involves the use of a heavy object, such as a log or rock, balanced upon a triggering device which, when touched by an animal, allows the heavy object to drop and trap or outright kill the animal.

Deadfalls are not practical for anyone but the most ardent do-it-yourselfer. They are extremely time-consuming to construct, non-selective and simply inefficient when compared to the modern traps, whether leghold, killer, or live-box variety. Nonetheless, the accompanying illustrations are examples of deadfalls that are well tried and comparatively productive. They are supplied for the benefit of the diehard purist who insists upon making his own traps and yet is not willing to mine iron ore and puddle the necessary steel to make legholds.

One final word about deadfalls is appropriate. Other than concern about the suffering of *any* animal trapped, the biggest criticism of trapping is that nontarget animals are injured or killed by nonselective traps. The deadfall is preeminently nonselective and has been outlawed in many jurisdictions. A trapper would be wise to consult his conscience and his local game code before setting any deadfalls.

Deadfalls

Steel Traps

Steel traps are, of course, the backbone of the fur trapping industry. Without the relatively lightweight, easy-to-carry steel leghold or killer-type traps, trapping necessarily would be confined to easily accessible spots where the far more expensive and infinitely clumsier live traps or colony traps could be used since managing many of these traps is simply impossible. Trapping beaver would be virtually impossible as would effective control — other than with poison — of many or most other furbearers.

Some trappers who have seen antitrappers bring pressure to bear against the steel leghold trap and land sets of body-gripping traps have become more or less fatalistic about trapping as it is known today, that is, with steel traps as the mainstay. The suggestion has been made that trappers had better get used to the idea of lugging clumsy traps about, since public opinion is bound to become sufficiently negative toward the leghold to result in its being outlawed. But, so long as public acceptance of the steel trap continues at the present level, the steel trap will remain the trapper's mainstay.

The steel traps fall rather conveniently into two major categories with subvarieties: (1) the steel leghold with its coil spring and long spring styles; (2) the killer types—more appropriately called humane traps.

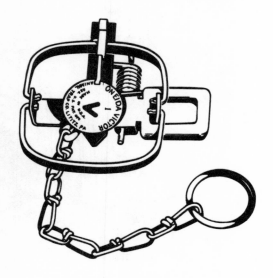

Steel leghold trap

A few words about the makeup of a steel trap: There are no jagged teeth that some cartoons and antitrappers choose to picture. The fact is that nearly all jurisdictions have explicitly outlawed steel traps without smooth jaws, and this illegalization has led to the virtual extinction of any type other than the smooth-jawed trap. It should be emphasized for the benefit of nontrappers, that the steel leghold traps are designed to do just that — hold the leg. The steely-jawed horror antitrappers point to would be better termed amputation or laceration traps.

The leghold traps all employ the same principle, namely a spring device compressed and held in suspension by a lever or levers against steel jaws and a trigger attached to a release, or pan. When the pan is touched by an animal, the trigger is released, breaking the restraint on the springs, which forces the jaws up and, in turn, closed.

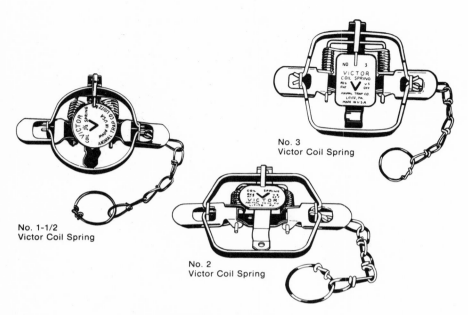

No. 1-1/2
Victor Coil Spring

No. 3
Victor Coil Spring

No. 2
Victor Coil Spring

Coil spring and jump traps

The coil spring and jump varieties of the leghold traps are favored by trappers because they are compact. Narrow cubbies and close-fitting log openings are no problem with these traps because the springs supplying the power to close the jaws are under the pan and beneath the jaws — very compact and convenient. Many trappers have in the past considered these traps somehow too small and flimsy for larger animals, since the size, weight, and general appearance of the traps is not so imposing as the cousin long-spring leghold trap. However, on a drowning set or even a land set, jump and coil-spring traps are just as tenacious as the long spring. In fact, many trappers prefer the more compact traps because the closed traps hold the foot higher and more completely shielded from the furbearer and therefore can eliminate the animal mutilating its own leg in an attempt to escape.

The long-spring trap or the larger double long-spring trap are the more common and in some cases sturdier leghold traps. Most beaver trappers who use a leghold trap, even without a drowning set, use a No. 3 double spring for its weight and its ineffable holding ability. The long spring's relative size creates a problem mitigated to some extent by the spring being angled around or against the set jaws.

Two improvements on the basic leghold trap deserve special mention. The "stop loss" or "sure grip" is an improved leghold trap that has a heavy wire bail that serves as a third jaw. When the trap is sprung, the two true jaws snap shut and the bail snaps down at right angles to them. The bail pins the animal or kills it outright, thereby eliminating gnawing or wring-offs. The other improvement is the double-jaw leghold, which is simply a trap with parallel jaws on each side. The double jaw also prevents gnawing or wring-off.

Long spring leghold trap

Many trappers who can remain objective suggest the jump trap versus long-spring trap question is merely a matter of taste. An objective study does tend to support this although the controversy is not reduced by the suggestion that there is no difference. The suggestion leads to there being three positions instead of two. One trapper of considerable experience clung to the position that the long spring was a superior holding trap despite evidence to the contrary. When confronted with the studies, he said he was aware of the tests but defended his position. He compared the difference to standing in the middle of the highway where a person would get hit by traffic going in both directions.

Killer Types
The killer-type trap is often termed the trappers' salvation by students of the art, simply because the killer trap does not lend itself to

the scene of an animal struggling against the leghold trap. This is the type of scene that the antitrapping fraternity finds so heartrending. On the other hand, improperly placed killer traps can expose some fairly hair-raising scenes. Worse yet, a killer trap set on land can lead to disaster if a domestic animal wanders into it. Consequently, some jurisdictions have outlawed the killer trap and many others have severely limited or prohibited its use other than in water.

No. 220-2 Conibear

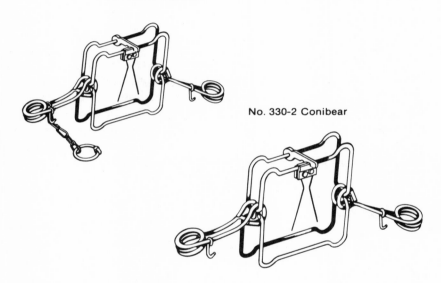
No. 330-2 Conibear

Killer or conibear trap

This killer-type trap — named for its principal developer — is commonly called the conibear. The trap has two solid steel wire frames that are opposed into an open, squared position against a spring and restrained by a dog attached to a trigger. Contact releases the spring's tension and reverses the frames, trapping whatever was unfortunate enough to touch the trigger.

The killer-type trap is favored by all trappers, especially for water sets with particular emphasis on beaver trapping. The one major drawback with the conibear trap is the likelihood of unwanted animals

27

wandering into the traps with catastrophic results. This, of course, virtually never happens with water sets. As a result, the larger-sized killer traps are never recommended for land sets and are flatly prohibited by law for such dry sets in many states. Missouri, for example, has followed a succession-to-extinction approach for the conibear. The recent skyrocketing prices for furs have intensified trapping pressure. This spiral, in turn, has led to proportionately more traps for progressively more domestic animals to blunder into. Missouri cut the size limitation on land set conibear traps from seven to five inches and also seriously considered forbidding a set other than in water unless the set was at least six feet above ground.

Snares

Snares have more or less fallen out of favor and are simply illegal in many jurisdictions. The disfavor is related to the relatively low productivity of snares and the fact that snared animals not properly captured can present the kind of dangling, pitiful sight which can raise antitrapping sentiment to a fever pitch. The illegality is based mostly upon the tendency of snares to be nonselective and to a lesser extent upon the improper snaring — or cruelty — problem.

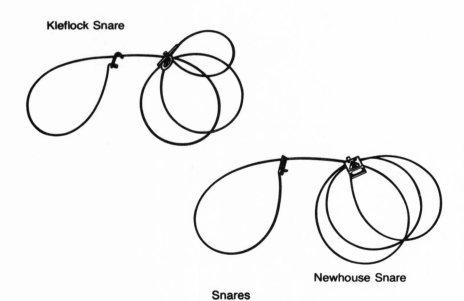

Kleflock Snare

Newhouse Snare

Snares

28

Snares do have their place, however. They are extremely compact and lightweight and can work as drowning sets almost as well as leghold traps or killer-type traps. Just for comparison, the author took eight Kleflock snares that would fit into a side coat pocket and compared the weight; the eight snares weighed the same as a No. 1½ long spring.

Some commercial suppliers make snares available. The Kleflock snare and Newhouse snare are both available from the Victor Company. They are inexpensive but difficult to find in retail stores and therefore should be ordered in advance of the season.

Actually, the enterprising trapper can make his own snares from a steel guitar string, a bit of putty or gum, and a fence staple to hold it in place. The end of the guitar string is threaded through the "spool" to make a loop, the staple is driven to hold the wire in place and the putty or gum holds the loop in the desired size. When an animal enters the snare, the gum or putty will slip away and allow a smooth tightening. Any wire can be fashioned to work in a similar way but nothing appears to be so easily put into service as a guitar string. The great difficulty in making a snare from stove wire, for example, is in making the end loop properly so that the noose will slide and close smoothly. All but the most ardent do-it-yourselfers will find the commercial snares far more satisfactory.

Snares are effective on animals that move in a predictable pattern, such as coyote, fox, or raccoon; lynx and bobcat also will fall prey to the snare. Water sets with snares also are effective, as runs can be located and snares placed in precise spots where the animals frequent. Bait or scent are rarely used with snares.

Live Traps

Live traps have their place in fur trapping, and, similar to all other traps, they have their advantages as well as their drawbacks.

No doubt the greatest advantage that the live trap has is that there is simply no carnage of nontarget animals. For that matter, there is no pain and suffering inflicted on target animals, either. The animal that happens into a live trap is simply confined and suffers no ill from the trap itself.

Any suggestion that there are disadvantages to using a live trap is certainly going to result in outcries of protest. Nonetheless, there are drawbacks to such traps. By comparison to steel traps, the live traps are bulky and relatively expensive. The effort involved in a single trapper

A beaver live-trapped for restocking. (courtesy J.E. Osman
and the Pennsylvania Game Commission)

handling, say, 50 or 60 live traps would simply be too much under most conditions. In addition, live traps cost a minimum of three times what a steel trap costs. Another, lesser problem with the live trap is precisely what to do with certain animals that are trapped. For example, no one has yet devised an appropriate way to handle a skunk caught in a live trap, especially if the trap is a box-type trap which cannot be seen into easily. Finally, one real disadvantage of the live trap is that it is highly visible; this leads to endless problems with passersby who see a trapped animal and take it upon themselves to release it and sometimes damage or steal the trap.

On balance, then, the live trap is extremely effective, if somewhat limited in use. Appropriate locations for live traps are relatively close to transportation and terrain that is fairly easy going. The furbearing animals most often taken in live traps are the skunk, raccoon, and occasionally the muskrat, mink, and weasel. Scents, lures, and baits used in other sets will work very well in the live set.

Killing animals caught in the live trap presents a problem, also. Companies that produce such traps have now stopped recommending drowning and have tended toward use of automotive exhausts. The most effective, obviously, is some sort of firearm.

The live trap does lend itself to the do-it-yourself instinct that so many trappers seem to have. Unlike the steel leghold or conibear, the live trap does not have complicated mechanisms or strong springs; the live trap operates on triggers being tripped and a gravity principle dropping doors into place. Consequently, reasonably effective live traps can be constructed fairly simply. As an example of how to make humane live traps, here are the dimensions for a small trap for possums, muskrats, mink, or skunks. First, cut the following sized pieces from scrap, ⅜" plywood:

2 - 21½" x 6" (top and bottom pieces)
2 - 22" x 7¼" (side pieces)
2 - 7" x ¾"
1 - 6¾" x 5½"
1 - 7¼" x 6¾"

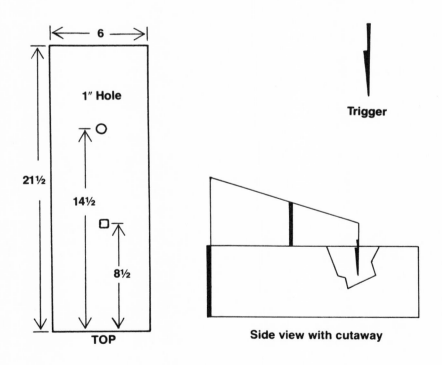

Do-it-yourself live trap

In addition, a ½" x ½" stick 15" long, a 1" x 5" stick and a ½" x ½" x 6" "trigger" are needed.

Center a 1" hole 14½" from the end of one of the 21½" pieces. Nail the 1" x 1" 5" stick on the end of the same piece centered 8½" from the end. This completes the top.

Attach the 22" x 7¼" boards to the top and bottom, squaring the ends nearest the 1" hole, to make a box 7¼" high and 6¾" wide. Close the end nearest the 1" hole with the 7¼" x 6¾" piece.

Attach one 7" x ¾" strip to each side of the mouth of the box to serve as facings for the 6¾" x 5½" door. Use monofilament fishing line to attach to the 15" stick which will serve as a lever to be balanced on the 5" fulcrum already nailed to the top. To the other end of the 15" stick, attach the notched trigger which will be balanced inside the 1" hole. An animal entering the box will touch the trigger which will allow the door to drop. The animal will be held unharmed.

Of course, the same sort of trap with larger proportions can be made for larger animals. Try sides of 36" x 11" x 11" for raccoons, 42" x 11" x 13" for bobcats and fox.

The larger sizes can become very heavy. Some trappers make frames in the proper dimensions and cover them with hardware cloth. Assembled in the proper way, the live trap will work very well and can be easily carried.

Special Treatment of Steel Traps

Dyeing and waxing traps is an annoyance and many trappers seek used traps to avoid this drudgery. Nonetheless, dyeing and waxing traps are essential steps in maximizing success with many furbearers and for preventing deterioration of the equipment from the unavoidable moisture and fluctuating temperatures. There is no substitute for these final preparatory steps; dyeing will disguise the traps and waxing will make the action quicker and to some extent deodorize — or at least substitute an odor — for maximum efficiency.

New traps are invariably covered with a light coating of machine oil from the manufacturer. This must be removed as a first step before dyeing; any lingering oily residue will result in the dye not setting properly and will leave shiny spots. This oil can be removed in at least three ways. First, the traps can be exposed to the elements for a few weeks. Second, they can be subjected to extreme heat such as a bonfire which will simply burn the oil off. Finally, they can be boiled in water until all of the oil has been freed and poured off. This final step can be good even with older traps as it will remove any lingering crud, oil, and wax from the previous season.

Most experienced trappers allow the traps to take on a fine coating of rust which is then wire-brushed off; the procedure takes a few days but will result in oil-free traps that will dye solid black promptly. One way of hastening the rusting process is to dip the oil-free traps in a strong salt solution.

Dyeing the traps is a simple, if time consuming, task. The jaws of the trap should be opened and a link of the chain placed between the jaws to hold them open so that even the jaw edges get dyed. The traps are dropped into a crock or cauldron containing a wood dye solution strong enough to float a horseshoe. The traps should remain in the dye at least one full week to assure a complete dyeing that is more than surface deep. Remove the traps and hang them outside to dry and deodorize for a day or two.

Some trappers enjoy making their own dyes by boiling walnut hulls and adding vinegar to the resulting stain. Excellent commercial dyes made from logwood, which both colors and lightly waxes traps, are widely available at very low cost. These should be considered by anyone with concern about time and neatness in dyeing.

Waxing is a final step considered by some trappers as frivolous and by others as essential to maintaining traps, assuring long life for equipment and permitting lightning-quick actions even when the trap is cold and slightly iced up. Waxing is commonly accomplished by lowering the trap by the chain into very hot paraffin; beeswax is better because of smell but is almost prohibitively expensive. The trap is held in the paraffin for at least a full minute to be certain that the trap has reached the temperature of the paraffin, thereby assuring the even coating needed, and then removed slowly and hung to dry. This paraffin treatment can be a trifle dangerous given the chances of flash fire, splattering, and boiling over. As a simplified way and a much safer technique, some trappers boil their traps and then add enough paraffin for two inches of melted paraffin on the surface of the water. When the traps are removed from their cleansing boil-bath, they are pulled slowly through the layer of paraffin on the surface and are thus coated with wax.

Some trappers have accepted advanced technology and have begun using the new acrylic floor plastics as an easier way to "wax" traps. These traps are dipped into the floor covering, removed, and allowed to dry; no heat is necessary and the coating is at least as effective as wax, if more expensive.

Still other trappers see nothing sacred in waxing and lubricate with animal fat or a spritz of WD-40, although the scent from the WD-40 is probably too strong and too foreign for the trapline and is therefore not recommended.

Whatever the choice of lubricants, something should be used on legholds to reduce friction after all of that exposure to weather, heat, and dyes.

Note: A conibear or killer-type trap should *never* be waxed. Conibears are used under different conditions from legholds and these differences reduce or eliminate the need for lubrication. More important, wax makes a conibear all but impossible to set. A trapper can acquire bent and broken fingers too easily with an unwaxed conibear trap without adding wax to assist in the job.

ACCESSORIES

Shovels

As the section on sets will make clear, efficient trapping requires a certain amount of earth moving—far too much for a knife blade or fingernails to handle. A trapper needs some sort of shovel. Since trapping requires moving considerable distances on foot and often over difficult terrain, the shovel needs to be lightweight and as compact as possible. A simple garden trowel is one answer; the trowel is the ultimate in compactness and can be carried in a jacket pocket. The only improvement to make on a trowel as it comes from the hardware store might be to drill a hole and run a leather thong through the handle to eliminate problems associated with the trowel being misplaced or ending up at the bottom of a creek after slipping from cold-stiffened hands. The trowel has only one real shortcoming: that very compactness makes it less than desirable for larger digging jobs and is of limited value for chiseling through frozen topsoil or breaking ice of any real thickness.

By far the best trapper's shovel is the military device called the entrenching tool or fox hole shovel. This little shovel has a total length of 28 inches when extended and has a wide blade for digging dirt-hole sets; the shovel also has a foot edge to make pushing easier. In addition, the entrenching tool has the weight necessary for swing leverage and can be useful for breaking ice or any other use as a club. A unique feature of this shovel is that the blade angle may be adjusted up to 180 degrees,

Fox hole shovels

from flat against the handle (thereby reducing the overall length considerably) to fully extended. By stopping midway and tightening the threaded clamp, the shovel can be converted into a pick of sorts, especially useful for hacking, grubbing, or clearing on the trapline. The size of the fox hole shovel makes it useful as a club for killing captured furbearers. The additional length and weight of this shovel need not be too much of an annoyance; when the blade is clamped flat against the handle, the overall length is only 21 inches. Blade cases that belt the shortened shovel to the trapper are available at a nominal price.

Newer military entrenching tools have a pick blade in addition to the shovel edge. One variety has a collapsible metal handle; the entire tool is less than 10 inches long and can be tucked into a canvas case. The several varieties of entrenching tools are widely available at many surplus outlets, gardening centers, and discount houses.

Sifter
A sifter is a frame with coarse hardware cloth stretched over it. The device is used to crumble and scatter dirt and snow on a set to make it more natural looking and to cover the trap without leaving large pieces that might hamper the action of the jaws. Obviously, the sifter is of very limited value to the trapper who confines his efforts mostly to water sets, and all trappers can get by without one. But given the usefulness of the

A sifter helps disguise sets.

36

sifter and the ease with which it can be made, most trappers make and carry one. To make a sifter, construct a 10-by-10-inch frame of 1-by-1-inch wood stock, cover the frame with hardware cloth and reinforce as needed with strips of wood. The trapper can easily construct a sifter, or one may be purchased fairly inexpensively from most trapper supply houses.

Wire

An accessory that may well be considered an integral part of the trap is wire used to anchor the trap or connect it to a drag. Wire can be a bother — heavy, hard to sraighten and bend — but it is a necessary annoyance. The temptation to use light, compact, easy to cut and attach nylon line is great, but should be resisted; the nylon can fall prey to the teeth and claws of furbearers. This results in lost traps and animals that "escape" to die in the lair, a total loss to all concerned. Coils of stove wire are available at any hardware store for about a dollar. Most trappers of experience carry the entire coil afield and reduce the wire to usable size as needed. This necessitates some cutting but is far, far less cumbersome than trying to carry traps with lengthy wires attached, especially in brushy country. Custom cutting also eliminates the too short drag wire.

Stove wire can be broken by repeated, fast opposing bends until the metal fatigues and snaps. The already heavily burdened trapper may be tempted to forego wire clippers to reduce the load. This technique will work, of course, but small, lightweight clippers can be well worth the extra weight. The cutters will part wire much faster and can be used to wrap the wire properly even when cold or wet fingers do not respond well. Furthermore, when the time comes to move a trap, the drag wire can be clipped easily without causing disturbance. Several models of cutters are available widely and the choice is one of taste and price.

Bags

Bags are sometimes overlooked by trappers but they can be very useful in preparation, in the field, and after pelt removal. As explained in the pelt preparation and care section, many fur buyers accept or even prefer pelts that are frozen raw; this saves a lot of time and effort for trappers with freezer space — and bags — in which to store the season's catch prior to sale. Since each animal pelt should be kept separately bagged, this practice can require many bags.

In addition to bagging pelts and carcasses, otherwise messy baits such as fat or grease, stink baits, chunks of wild meat, and soft fruits can be carried — or for that matter gathered afield — easily in plastic bags.

Plastic bags in which bread and rolls are packaged are perfect for most of these uses; the larger ones will hold a cut-up carcass for freezing. Stuffed one into another, these bags are extremely light and compact. Best of all, they are free. A trapper anticipating a good season can collect these bags year-round to insure an adequate supply during the season.

The small, clear plastic bags known as sandwich bags also are useful for individual baits such as frozen sardines or bits of furbearer entrails. These bags are very inexpensive and may be reused indefinitely.

Ax or Hatchet

A hand ax or hatchet can be extremely useful on a trapline for chopping stakes, making drags, driving nails or staples, scraping, hacking, or even makeshift grubbing or digging. Any ax or hatchet will do, of course, but probably the best is a scout type with a belt holster.

Kneeling Sheet

A simple device for minimizing the human scent and keeping the trapper's knees dry is the kneeling sheet — a plastic sheet spread on the ground for the trapper to kneel on while the set is being made. Use of a kneeling sheet does seem to make a noticeable difference in catches of furbearers such as coyotes, which are especially sensitive to human smell. The sheet can also be used to haul away excess dirt and ground cover. The kneeling sheet need not be anything elaborate, just a heavy-duty plastic sheet which can be folded and tucked into a pocket. Probably the best and most readily available is a plastic leaf bag. But to kneel or not to kneel is a question raised later in the section on sets.

Wading Stick

A wading stick can be invaluable to the trapper who can find the extra hand to carry one. For some reason, trappers and especially beginning trappers seem to think there is some shame in using an extra leg to keep their balance. But when one learns of the great advantage in carrying the "spare leg," it suddenly becomes essential equipment, especially for the water trapper. A broom or mop handle four or more

Construction of a set using a kneeling sheet. (courtesy J.E. Osman and the Pennsylvania Game Commission)

feet long, fitted with a thong for easy gripping, is best. Many trappers add a screw-in hook to one end; this hook can be used to grope for trap wires, traps, and drowning cords in water sets.

Basket

A trapper's basket is a very useful accessory because it can free the hands for other tasks and also distribute a great deal of weight to the back and legs where it can be handled easily. These baskets can be used to lug furbearers, extra traps, bait, or anything else that will fit. They are large and usually open-ended backpack-type devices. The trapper's-basket is available commercially from several sources. Some trappers devise their own from small laundry hampers and sturdy backpack straps.

Trapper's Tool

As occasionally happens, a tool that will do the work of several others has been invented. Not too cleverly named the trapper's tool, the device is a combination knife, hatchet, entrenching tool, and hammer.

The trapper's tool is available in various sizes and is for the trapper who would rather spend money than lug several tools.

Scrapers

Scrapers are tools used to remove fat and flesh from the hide of pelts. A keen edge is definitely not recommended for scraping, as cuts and slices in a pelt will reduce its value. A knife with an edge no sharper than a smooth butter knife is acceptable. A putty knife or scraper will work. The "hog scraper" is probably the best tool available.

Lantern

Some sort of illumination almost certainly will be needed. Trappers should be at the traps early enough to clear populated areas before attracting a crowd and to prevent any charges of long, lingering stays in the traps. A three-, four-, or five-cell flashlight will work well as will the nine-volt seal beam lights that are so popular. The lantern illustrated has

Peak 1 compact lantern (courtesy Coleman Company)

at least two advantages. First, the fuel is relatively cheap and may be replaced at any service station. Second, the lantern casts illumination in a much larger area, which makes working in the dark somewhat more like working by day.

Trap Setters and Things

The outdoor gadget that is worth having around is rare indeed. Three such items have recently become available for trappers.

The first is called a jiffy trap setter and allows a trapper to set the stubbornest long spring with one hand as it compresses the spring in a plier-like fashion. Not only does this device eliminate stumbling about trying to compress the spring with a foot but it is also much faster.

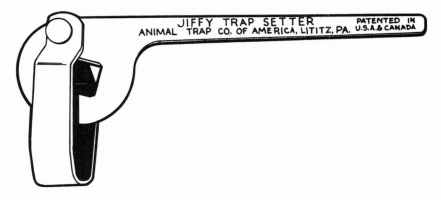

Jiffy trap setter (courtesy Woodstream Corporation)

The second is a long-handled device that permits the trapper to set a conibear trap with ease. This is a very useful tool, since a conibear can be tricky when warm and dry but can be next to impossible to set when wet and/or cold.

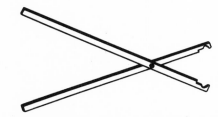

Conibear trap setter (courtesy Woodstream Corporation)

The third specialty item also relates to the conibear and may be a godsend. The device, called the conibear safety gripper, is a clamp that holds the jaws open, and makes an accidental triggering of the trap impossible. This is an extremely valuable safety feature as anyone who has ever been nipped by a conibear will agree.

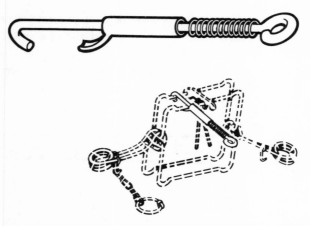

Conibear safety gripper (courtesy Woodstream Corporation)

Knives

The trapper without a knife is akin to a fisherman without one. A trapper simply does not realize how frequently a knife is used until it is left behind or lost. Cutting guide stakes, scratching crud from traps, cutting bait, makeshift shoveling, enlarging a hole planned for a blind set, or anything needing scraping, prying, or cutting are just some of the uses afield for a knife. The best knife for the job or jobs is largely one of personal preference.

A trapper can probably get by with any bargain-counter piece of junk that can take an edge and keep it. And, doubtless a number do just that. However, a great many trappers choose to look at the knife as an investment, a tool, and do not scrimp on cost, whether the choice be a pocketknife or sheath knife.

Actually, the term pocketknife is not all that accurate these days. A great number of the folding-type knives are far too large to be pocketed and end up in a sheath — a holster, really — on the belt. The folding knife fans appreciate the compactness and common availability of a second or even third blade; it is similar to having two knives.

For sheath knife fans — those who like the rigid blade of what was once called a hunting knife — the lines and quick availability of the steel without fumbling to expose the blade more than make up for the fact that there is only *one* blade. Properly chosen, the single blade will perform all required functions without any need for a second blade.

Several companies offer splendid knives for the trapper. Some even have cutesy slogans such as "for skinning a small squirrel or a large elephant." Among the knives made especially for trappers are those with a drop point; this type of knife has the blade curve reversed so that skinning can be done quickly and without so much danger of penetrating the carcass. Trappers who favor a pocketknife can choose among the two- and three-bladed pocketknives known as the muskrat or improved muskrat.

The Diamondback (courtesy Benchmark Knives)

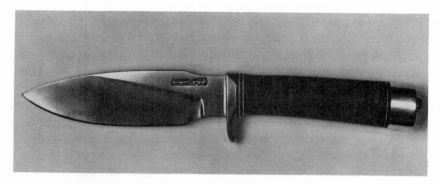

The handcrafted Alaskan Skinner, one of the first drop point knives made. (courtesy Randall Made Knives)

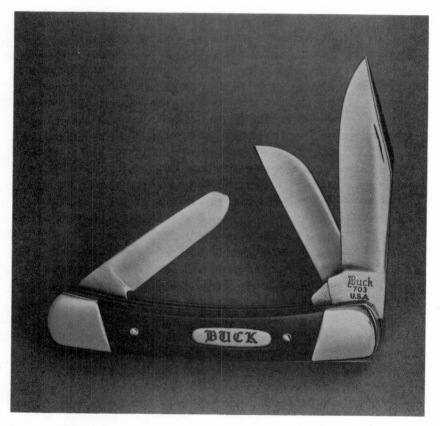

The Colt folding knife (courtesy Buck Knives)

An assortment of drop point folding knives (courtesy Buck
Knives)

Buck skinning knives (courtesy Buck Knives)

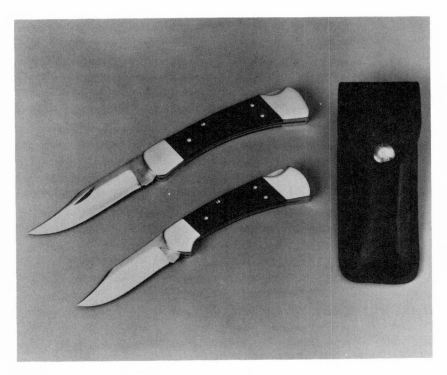

Buck folding sheath knives (courtesy Buck Knives)

Firearms

A firearm of some kind is necessary to any trapper for killing larger trapped animals and the occasional problem catch. For example, a skunk can be a problem under the best circumstances and can be a really tough customer when handled with a stick rather than the comfortable distance a gun can provide.

Probably the best choice for trappers is a .22 handgun with shorts or the mighty midget called the CB cap. Handgun laws being what they are, the more likely, available choice is the .22 rifle similarly loaded. In either case, the trapper should use solid point ammunition rather than the extraordinarily expanding hollow points. These hollow points have their place in hunting, of course, but in trapping the shots are extremely controlled, and often at very close range. Besides, the hollow point is designed to expand and do a great deal of damage, which is precisely what the trapper needs to avoid.

In addition to the greater potential damage they can do to the pelt, hollow points simply do not have the accuracy expected from a solid point even at close range. The .22 short is the best choice; it has plenty of power for trapping duties and yet is nowhere near as loud as the larger charges. This little bullet may well have been designed for trappers, as it is inexpensive and very accurate for short distances. Some recent ballistics tests seem to indicate that the .22 long is not well balanced between weight and power, resulting in comparative inaccuracy. The .22 long rifle is balanced, as is the .22 short, and is therefore highly accurate but is far too powerful for many of the extremely close shots.

An interesting alternative to the .22 rimfire is the compressed air rifle or pellet gun. The need for power can be satisfied by the variety of rifles that work from the lever-action compressing air. The rifles manufactured by Benjamin, Crosman, and Sheridan in either .22 caliber or, in the case of the Sheridan, 5 mm, can deliver all of the power necessary at extremely low cost; the ammunition runs less than one half cent per shot with elbow grease providing the power. The CO_2 versions of the air rifle are not recommended because the power of such weapons drops from shot to shot which, to say the least, is not desirable. The trapper who fires a dozen shots in a day has had an exceptional day, so the bit of pumping involved is not that big a problem.

The air rifle can deliver all the firepower a trapper needs at these extremely limited ranges. For example, the Benjamin No. 342 .22-caliber rifle produces 750 FPS, which is more than adequate. For that matter, the pump pellet pistol is sufficient and much more compact; the Benjamin No. 132 .22-caliber pistol delivers 500 FPS.

The Benjamin Model 342 air rifle — a nonpowder alternative for the trapper. (courtesy Benjamin Air Rifle Company)

The Model 132—the alternative sidearm. (courtesy Benjamin
Air Rifle Company)

One real advantage to an air rifle choice is that the nonpowder-
driven guns do not usually carry with them the sort of stigma attached
to firearms. There is no report of any consequence from the release of air
which drives the pellet, and the gun-regulating people, at the time of this
writing, have not made acquisition of these weapons too difficult.

If a rifle is the choice rather than a handgun, the trapper may want
to consider a sling to carry the firearm easily and yet keep the hands free
for the other tasks of trapping. Straps that can be adapted to nearly any
rifle are available at nominal costs from military surplus stores.

BAIT

Baits are a part of trapping almost as certainly as are traps
themselves. Something of a scent or taste to lure the furbearer close to
the set and, finally, onto the trap pan can greatly increase the season's
catch. Baits also reduce fear of sets by distracting the furbearer. Baits
break more or less conveniently into three categories: natural, processed,
and scents, also known as lure.

Natural Baits
Natural baits may be something of a misnomer as *all* furbearer baits
are natural. For purposes of making this distinction, natural baits are
not smoked, pickled, distilled, rendered, or otherwise processed.

High on the list of natural fruit baits are persimmons. Opossums love them, raccoons will forage for them, and muskrats also can be lured with them. They also have the advantage of being widely available during most of the trapping season. Several pounds, preferably in small quantities divided among numerous bags, can be used throughout the season for baited sets. For the sake of neatness, a trapper should gather firm persimmons, but damaged or even mashed fruit will work.

Other fruits and vegetables can be used as bait and can be equally good for muskrats. Good choices include apples, turnips, parsnips, carrots, and raw potatoes. Carry these afield whole and cut or break into pieces as needed.

Honey, another excellent natural bait, is treated in greater detail in the section on lures for reasons that will be seen.

Raw meat products such as suet or simple fatty scraps also are available cheap or free from obliging meatcutters. Carcasses or skinned furbearers can be a source of natural bait as well. Squirrel, rabbit, and woodchuck or groundhog will do nicely. Use entrails from any of these as gob baits. Chop pieces of carcass the size of stew meat for bait; if feasible, leave the hair or fur on the bait. Any type of this raw meat will attract possums, raccoons, mink, coyotes, wolves, fisher, marten, bobcat, and the occasional weasel.

Minnows are exceptionally good natural baits for use on traplines that run along water. Since the minnows will ordinarily be in a bait-hole set, they obviously need not be fresh. Minnows often are available free for the asking — a few at a time — as dead minnows are discarded at bait shops; many trappers pick these freebies up as they become available during the season and save them for trapping. The minnows sold in little jars at bait shops will work, also.

If necessary, all natural baits can be preserved by freezing. In all cases, the best approach is to freeze a quantity that will serve as one bait, thereby avoiding the problem of chiseling a small bait from a large frozen chunk. Half a dozen persimmons is about right for a persimmon set; two or three minnows is sufficient. Other fruits and vegetables can be acquired fresh as needed or frozen when abundant.

Meat and entrails can present something of a problem in that such baits are often best when slightly tainted. The question here is how to have tainted meat and keep it, too. A common practice is to taint the chunks and gobs by placing them in a sealed plastic bag at a temperature warm enough to promote decomposition and then freezing the bait, bag, and all, when the process should be arrested. The bait is then thawed the night before being set out or simply carried frozen to the field. In either case, the bag is left intact until the set is in place and the bait ready to be placed. Special care should be taken to avoid accidents with the tainted baits, and an extra plastic bag should be carried afield to carry back the emptied bait bags.

Processed Baits

Many processed baits are available from the most ordinary places. A few pieces of well-smoked bacon or bacon rind, whether or not tainted, will work well to attract all of the carnivorous furbearers. Sardines are especially good for raccoons, mink, and marten. All cooked, fragrant meat scraps such as skins from cooked turkey, cooked bacon rind, fat, ham, and corned beef will lure in roaming animals.

The canned meat and fish products can, of course, be kept tinned until baiting. All of the others will freeze well for preservation. Renderings — both hard "cracklings" and soft fats or lard — from meats will make good bait.

Lure (Scents)

People can easily overlook the value of the scent of bait since the sense of smell is ordinarily not very well developed in humans, or if it is well developed, it is stunned by the constant assault of perfumes and other odors. Surrounded as we are by the powerful smells from cooking, smoking, industrial and vehicle fuels, and even room fresheners and deodorants, we are often unaware of the olfactory sense. Animals, on the other hand, are acutely aware of smells and especially those coming from food or, in the trapper's case, bait. In addition, furbearing animals see everything as black, white, or shades of gray. Since this is so, the sense of smell takes on a greatly added significance.

Commercially prepared lure is available in sporting goods stores and by mail. They are inexpensive, attractively packaged, and small supplies will last the most vigorously energetic trapper a full season. Far more important, lure often produces the most overpoweringly nauseating odors imaginable in confined areas. A few drops of rancid fish oil or concentrated animal urine in a house will make the smell of burning chicken feathers seem pleasant by comparison. Therefore, it is earnestly recommended that trappers refrain from making their own lure and resort instead to commercial products.

Having said that, the following recipes are offered for those financially strapped enough, possessed of enough do-it-yourself instinct, or simply hardheaded enough to be determined to go it alone.

Badger lure

In a pint jar, mix equal amounts of beaver castor, muskrat musk, and badger musk; add mineral oil to make the mixture fluid and allow to age for two weeks. Use sparingly around dirt-hole sets and den sets.

Beaver lures

1. In a pint jar, mix two ground beaver castors, one half teaspoon anise oil, and enough mineral oil to make it liquid.
2. In a pint jar, mix equal amounts of beaver castor and beaver oil with a touch of oil of catnip or oil of birch and enough mineral oil to make a heavy liquid.

Use the above sparingly at slide sets and sets around heavily worked timbered areas.

Bobcat lures

1. Oil of catnip.
2. Equal amounts of whatever musk is available (otter, mink, muskrat, badger) mixed with mineral oil and a touch of catnip.
3. Beaver castors ground up and mixed with any musk and bobcat urine.

Use the above sparingly around baited cubby sets.

Coyote lures

1. Rancid fish oil mixed with any musk and coyote urine.
2. Rotted meat mixed with muskrat musk.

Fisher lure

In a quart jar, mix one half pint rancid fish oil with any musk plus one half teaspoon of anise; use around any baited set.

Fox lure

1. In a quart jar, mix four ounces of rancid fish oil, one ounce muskrat or beaver musk, two ounces of fox urine and allow to age.
2. Break two eggs lightly into a quart jar (shells and all) and allow to rot.

Use the above two lures at any fox set.

Marten lure

Mix two ounces of mineral oil with one ounce of rancid fish oil plus marten musk; use with any baited set for marten.

Mink lures

1. Mix rancid fish oil with any combination of musks.
2. Mix mineral oil with beaver castor or any musk.
3. Mix mineral oil with beaver castor and anise oil.

Use the above sparingly at any baited set for mink.

Muskrat lures

1. Mix one ounce each beaver castor and muskrat musk with one half teaspoon oil of catnip.
2. Mix one half teaspoon of anise oil with the grated peeling of an orange and enough mineral oil to make it all liquid.

Use the above sparingly on floating sets or other baited sets.

Raccoon lures

1. Add one half teaspoon each anise oil and oil of catnip to four ounces of honey.
2. Add one ounce of rancid fish oil to one teaspoon of beaver castor and one ounce of honey.

Use at any baited set for raccoon.

Weasel lures

1. Cheap perfume, any scent.
2. Rancid fish oil mixed with any musk or beaver castor.

Use the above with the box cubby set for weasel.

Of course, no one ever admits to setting traps for skunk or possum, but if anyone wanted to they could use the following lures:

Possum lures

1. Rancid fish oil.
2. Any musk.

Skunk lures

1. Lightly break two eggs, shell and all, into a pint jar and allow to ripen.
2. Honey with any musk.

While other means of attracting animals can be employed and might properly be called baits (for example, see the wing set and shiny object sets) we speak here of things that are generally considered food and that are scented to attract furbearers. Since the scent of bait is a function of volatility and volatility is in turn a function of moisture, the trapper must be careful to use only those baits that are moist. Dried-out baits should be replaced regularly by moist, highly scented baits.

CLOTHING

A trapper's clothing — his rig — should largely be a matter of taste tempered with common sense. Obviously, a Louisiana muskrat trapper will not need the heavy-duty warm clothing that a Minnesota nimrod needs. Likewise, a trapper planning on all dry-land sets in woodlands will not require the chest waders or hip boots that the water-set trapper needs. Nonetheless, some generalizations can be made and adapted to locality.

Gloves
A pair of gloves — and preferably two pairs — is a must for trapping. A warm pair is essential. The modern, down-filled gloves with water repellent covering are a good choice. The more readily available and cheaper fur-lined leather gloves will do the job although a little moisture on that fur can end up as ice or, nearly as bad, simple dampness that will chap hands so badly that the term "raw hide" will take on new meaning.

A pair of rubber gloves is nearly a necessity for the trapper who is going to use best efforts to keep human scents away from the sets. As the section on sets notes, the human scent can affect the catch, especially of trap-wary quarry such as mink; one way to reduce the human scent is to wear rubber gloves when actually making or baiting the set. The so-called living gloves marketed by Playtex are suitable since they permit nearly the same dexterity as bare hands while masking odor and/or keeping the hands dry when making water sets.

An interesting compromise between rubber gloves and gloves for warmth is now available: warm gloves covered with the thin plastic gloves used by cafeteria workers who touch foods with their hands. The regular gloves keep the hands warm and the plastic gloves shield odor and keep the hands (as well as gloves) dry. These plastic gloves are inexpensive and are available at many groceries and most drug stores.

Footwear.

The other extremities — the feet — are another matter. Once again, the weather conditions will largely dictate the choice; the land trapper has a far easier decision than the water-set trapper assuming, of course, the wet trapper goes afoot.

Good footwear is essential. The great distances to be walked and the rough terrain involved necessitate sturdy footwear with good ankle support and soles that help cushion the pounding, punishing impact. The boots marketed by Redwing and Wolverine have been favorites for decades because of the solid craftsmanship employed and the quality materials matched for performance. A good pair of leather boots with eight- to ten-inch tops and one-piece rubber soles will last for years even in the damp, spongy trapping grounds, assuming proper maintenance with available leather conditioners.

The water-set trapper has the problem of how to stay dry and relatively warm while walking in mud and water to set traps. This, of course, requires some sort of waterproof foot and legwear. The question becomes: hip boots or chest-high waders? Hip boots have the advantage of being easily pulled on and off; they actually can be worn as land boots also, and some fairly foolhardy trappers use hip boots almost like cowboy chaps, crashing through brush, a practice that is *not* recommended. On the other hand, hip boots are protections from the sole of the foot upward approximately two and one half feet; the trapper who steps into mud and water with a combined depth of 30¼ inches might as well be wearing jeans for all the good those hip boots are going to do. Stepping over the tops is never going to be popular and is almost guaranteed not to be habit-forming.

The alternative is chest waders. Big and bulky and a real hardship on land, they can permit a trapper to walk right down the middle of a stream or impoundment several feet deep. The trapper who can organize his line to get all water sets in a compact area without mixing in land movement will do well to choose chest waders. There are several types of chest waders available that are relatively light and almost like a plastic body stocking. These, of course, require shoes over the wader's feet; they may be a good choice if for no other reason than their lightweight compactness. The best footwear to put over these chest waders are the felt-soled trout fisherman's shoes; other than these, old tennis shoes with crepe soles will give surefootedness even in slippery streams.

Body Wear

For covering the body — legs and trunk — most trappers choose something like jeans and a flannel shirt with a foundation of insulated underwear if the conditions call for it. This attire permits a good range of movement, is unquestionably available at any time without special thought or preparation and, when augmented by a jacket or coat, provides adequate pocket space to hold all the odds and ends a trapper needs or thinks he will need.

For very cold weather trapping, insulated coveralls are becoming very popular. These overalls can replace the coat, the insulated undergarments, the hat and, for that matter, everything except footwear and gloves. They can be found in various weights including cold weather motorcycling sets, which fairly ignore extreme cold and chill factors. Some trappers jokingly say that these overalls are dangerous because they are so snugly warm that the only unprotected part — the face — can become numb while the rest of the body feels just fine; the trapper may well have a smile frozen on his face. The hood that comes with a set of these coveralls is a mixed blessing. The parka-type headgear with drawstring can keep the entire head and neck covered and warm, a very important factor, since over half the body heat loss escapes from the uncovered head and neck. However, this sort of headgear severely limits peripheral vision and reduces hearing acuity.

A final word about coveralls: Trappers should be aware of the reduced agility that comes from wearing coveralls. The stride is shortened; distances requiring a hop before now need a jump, a jump becomes a real effort and the long jump can fall short and become a head-over-heels tumble.

About smell and clothing: Trappers need to keep the scent problem in mind at all times. Human scent can reduce a catch to nothing. To minimize scent, many trappers keep trapping clothes separate from all others and even store them away from the house with its cooking odors, smoke, and room fresheners.

PELTS

With the first successes of the trapping season, there comes a need for additional equipment to handle the pelts. This equipment can be broken into two categories: stretching equipment and freezing equipment.

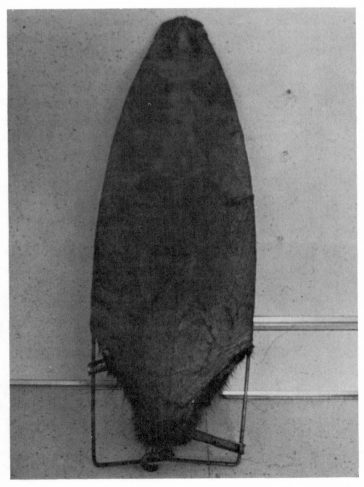

Wire stretchers hasten the drying process for the muskrat pelt.

Stretching Equipment

As the sections on individual furbearers indicate, most animals are case skinned rather than skinned open. However, individual fur buyers have different ideas on the subject and it will pay to make regular contact with the proposed fur buyer to learn his preference. The popularity of case skinning means that the trapper may need stretching boards or wire stretchers for drying pelts. Wooden stretchers look something like miniature ironing boards and may be fashioned from any scrap wood. The accompanying chart indicates the recommended sizes for each of the various species. If the proper thickness — or rather, thinness — of wood is available, using two very thin stretchers with a small separating wedge is recommended. The thin stretching makes it possible to use two stretchers at once. The two stretchers are put in place with the wedge between. When the pelt is cured, the wedge is removed, allowing the pelt to be slipped from the stretcher very easily. Another type of stretcher that is less common is the so-called Canadian type, a three-piece stretcher. The two larger pieces are inserted and the third, smaller piece is shoved between them to bring the pelt to the proper tension.

Canadian-type stretcher

58

Raccoon on a wooden stretching board. (courtesy
Mark Brown)

Wire stretchers, commonly referred to as fur-drying frames, are available commercially or can be fashioned from wire coat hangers. Many fur buyers have a marked preference for pelts dried on the wire stretchers because of the resulting flatness and uniformity of the pelts. The wire stretchers are unquestionably more compact to use as the pelts are tightened to a thickness of one half inch or less, depending on the pelt. The wire frames also have hooks on their bases for the added convenience of hanging the curing pelts on a wire, out of harm's way.

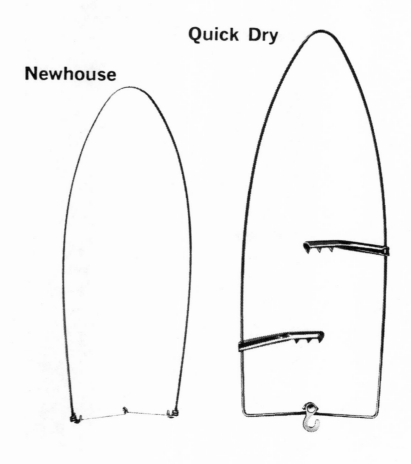

Wire stretchers come in several styles. (courtesy of Woodstream Corporation)

Salt

Salt is something about which trappers disagree. Some trappers use salt to hasten the curing process. Salt is added to the raw pelt to draw out moisture and loosen flesh which needs to be scraped from the pelt. Many trappers counsel against this practice, saying it damages the pelt by this speeding of the curing process. The question remains open as some trappers continue to maintain a small keg of iodine-free salt to sprinkle on raw pelts.

Scrapers

Scraping will require a dull blade. Dull knives are never hard to find or maintain. A smooth-bladed butter knife or even a teaspoon will suffice.

Freezing Equipment

Freezing equipment is just a long way of saying freezer. Use of freezing as a temporary expedient has been around trapping for decades. Whenever a trapper had more animals than he could stretch and cure, or skin at one time, he would resort to freezing the pelt or the entire animal until the time was available. Now many trappers are using the freezer as a substitute rather than a delay for stretching and drying. The animal is skinned and the pelt is dropped into a plastic bag without further treatment and is frozen until time for marketing. In certain places, fur buyers actually seem to prefer the frozen pelts. A discussion with the buyer may well pay off in time saved and money earned. The normal procedure is to allow the pelts to thaw enough to be examined by the buyer on the market day.

The freezer need not be anything special or elaborate. Many trappers use an old refrigerator set as low as it will register. This will work as well as a new deep freeze.

Tail Stripper

One small accessory that can be overlooked is a very inexpensive tool for stripping the tail from furbearers. Many trappers do without, while others use a couple of large nails clamped one on each side to slide the hide off. The accompanying illustration shows the best available strippers, a wooden device which slips over the inside of the tail and, maintaining consistent pressure on all points, allows the tail of the pelt to be slipped off. A crescent wrench also can be used for this purpose, and works very well as it contacts three sides of the tail and is adjustable to fit the size of whatever animal is being skinned.

Tail stripper

4 The Animals

Trapping is a specialized type of hunting which has as its object drawing the quarry to the point of capture. To maximize the chances of success at bringing the furbearers to the trap, the trapper needs as thorough as possible a knowledge of the animal's characteristics and habitat. As the primary predator of many furbearers, the trapper should know the reproduction capacity of each species so he can approach the maximum sustained yield on his traplines. The following are brief sketches of the characteristics of each of the furbearers commonly trapped in North America.

OPOSSUM

The opossum — or possum — has never received its due as a furbearer and perhaps never will. The possum has not even enjoyed a full share of the recent resurgence of interest in natural furs although the price of a possum pelt has risen enough to easily justify the time spent pelting the animals that are trapped. Despite this, no one seems willing to give this animal its due. Most people, trappers included, are even reluctant to call the possum's fur anything but hair, and many trappers flatly deny ever attempting to catch the possum deliberately.

The possum is the only North American marsupial, or pouched mammal. The possum young are born in a state which might be called premature in other animals. The blind, hairless newborn possums are about one half inch in length and will begin moving toward the mother's feeders almost as soon as emerging. The feeders number 13 and

The opossum — North America's only marsupial.

are in the mother's pouch. After eight to nine weeks, the babies will emerge from the pouch to ride on the mother's back, an intriguing sight. Ordinarily, six to nine survive to fend for themselves; they are weaned at three or four months whereupon a second litter is often conceived.

Mature possums will be from two to three feet in length including the tail and will weigh up to 14 pounds with the average around 9 pounds. Probably the most remarkable feature of the possum is the existence of "thumbs" on the hind feet which make the possum's track distinctive. Coupled with the possum's prehensile tail, the hind feet make the possum an almost unbelievably able climber. This climbing ability makes up for the possum's slowness afoot — the animal ambles along at less than one mile per hour and has a peak speed of less than five miles per hour, hardly more than a brisk walk for most large mammals. Other than climbing and other feats of hiding, the possum has a defense in the pungent odor about it. The smell resembles that of the skunk although it cannot be sprayed and does not begin to approach the skunk's intensity. Finally, a cornered possum may "defend" itself by feigning death, the famous "playing possum" trick — whether as an intentional act to avoid danger or from nervous paralysis — or it may stand its ground and fight. The possum is definitely not the pushover it appears to be at first. The few that stand their ground and fight have a very impressive arsenal. A possum's elongated face contains 50 needle-like teeth, the most of any North American mammal. Captured possums should be given all the respect ordinarily reserved for the furbearers considered more aggressive.

Possums are not specialized animals and will eat nearly anything. Therefore, they are found in great numbers in a vast expanse of North America and in nearly every type of terrain. In fact, some possums are actually trapped in large cities. For the most part, they eat insects, lizards, snails, toads, eggs, ground nesting birds, berries, mushrooms, and acorns. Possums like meat and, since they are slow-footed, seek carrion.

The possum has two redeeming characteristics that offset the relatively low value of the pelt: the meat is marketable and there are lots

The opossum possesses 50 needle-sharp teeth. (courtesy Mark Brown)

of them. The state of Louisiana publishes an annual report of furbearer harvest which in itself is not unusual, but it may be the only state that includes statistics on the numbers and values of the skinned carcasses sold. The possum harvest runs into many, many thousands of pounds which the Louisiana government estimates sells for 25 cents per pound. That figure is probably low as a random sampling in the Midwest and especially at well-established farmer's markets that set the price at more like $2.50 for a medium-sized possum carcass (around four pounds). That extra money is not a fortune, but it does bring the possum as a whole into a better position relative to other furbearers and may even price it as a major furbearer. The Missouri possum is considered by many to be the standard by which to measure. The average price for Missouri possum pelts in the late 1970s ran around $3.50 to $3.70. With the extra $2.50 for meat, the trapper would have a furbearer worth upwards of $6.

The sheer number of possums is impressive and, owing at least in part to the animal's total disregard for traps, catching six or seven or even more possums at a single set is not unusual. Reports of trappers at large garbage dumps taking 200 to 300 possums season after season are not unusual although the trappers will invariably deny seeking possums.

Possums are found nearly anywhere the surroundings have holes. Many are harvested from hollow trees or logs; abandoned groundhog holes harbor their share of possums as do old fox holes and small caves.

Although it is again noted that virtually no one ever acknowledges trapping for possums, just about any land set the trapper makes will take possum. Many smart trappers make sets for possums between sets for the more exotic species and thereby use all of the trapline.

Skinning and handling of pelts is discussed elsewhere, but one special comment about possums is necessary. Possums are easily the oiliest of the North American furbearers and pains should be taken to eliminate that oil quickly to reduce drying time. A thorough scraping after stretching will help, but it will often be necessary to wipe the oil away periodically to hasten drying. Special care should be taken on fleshing as the pouch of a possum will tear very easily.

WEASEL

The weasel is simply not the animal to be trapped at the time of this writing. Once one of the most highly prized pelts, especially in the

The least weasel — weighing less than one half pound.

winter form as ermine, and in great demand as material for the robes of royalty, the weasel currently is valued in most markets at less than one dollar per pelt. Then again, there are days within the memory of young men when fox pelts would not bring the price of shipping them and coyote was not even considered a furbearer. With the switch around in the market preferences possible at any time, the weasel may make a comeback as a major furbearer.

The weasel family includes skunk, mink, otter, badger, fisher, and marten, but here we discuss the true weasels. The weasels are easily the smallest commercially trapped furbearer. In fact, some weasels are so small that some old-timers talk about using a corncob as a stretching board for them. The diminutive size should not be misleading, however; the weasel is the consummate predator and is without fear. Weasels have an extraordinarily high metabolism that necessitates eating at frequent intervals with a consumption of 40 to 50 percent of the body weight in prey per day. Weasels will go after a remarkable number of food animals and, if pressed, will abandon the hunt for scarce prey of a reasonable size and go after prey many times its own size.

The least weasel is the world's smallest carnivore being six inches to nine inches in length including the tail and weighing approximately two ounces, hardly enough to be certain of tripping the most delicately set trap. Some least weasels turn white in winter. The ermine is the best known of these weasels and will measure 9 to 15 inches in length with a weight up to one-quarter pound. The furbearer's white color is a seasonal change from brown with a black tail tip. Long-tailed weasels will sometimes reach two feet in length and weigh up to one-half pound.

The weasel is fairly prolific, and the numbers of this furbearer occasionally make trapping it profitable. The home range of a weasel may be as much as 400 acres depending on species, but 20 or more may be found in a square mile of good habitat. Weasel dens are found in mixed territories and some will be taken on rocky, grown-up fence rows, meadows and even deep woods.

The size and market value of the weasel make the animal a less than primary trapping target. The best trap size for the weasel would be a No. 0 but that size is too small for any other furbearers and the weasel cannot really justify the effort as a target animal. Virtually all weasels are taken in No. 1 or No. 1½ traps or small killer traps set for other animals. A common mouse trap will work as a killer trap for weasels but has the obvious problem of constantly tempting mice.

Sets for weasel will seldom include bait except strictly fresh, bloody meat; the weasel prefers to catch its own prey and simply will not bait to what amounts to carrion. Weasels will lure to one type of scent; cheap perfume — the particular scent does not seem to matter — spritzed on and around a set can make it more attractive to weasels of all species. This, of course, can be disruptive to catches of the more valuable furbearers.

SKUNKS

Skunks are not at all closely related to opossums biologically, but as furbearers go, there is a definite kinship: both are prolific, well-known to all, and are scoffed if not outright shunned by trappers. Very few trappers will acknowledge any interest at all in the skunk aside from effort to keep the black-and-white animals *out* of their traps.

The two-striper, polecat, or just plain skunk. (courtesy Jay Kaffka)

Similar to opossums, most of the bad public relations is undeserved. Like all other furbearers, the skunk is a renewable resource; furthermore, it is both prolific and widely available to the trapper. The greatest shortcoming of the skunk is the relatively low price the pelts bring. The prices have been better — once again, *relatively* better — than in the past and have shown signs of improving recently, so this problem may correct itself as fashions change. Part of the market problem has always been that American fur wearers — the ultimate purchasers — have never appreciated the skunk as a furbearer and, as a result, all of the demand for skunk pelts has been from Europeans who do not share this prejudice. The demand for skunk seems to follow the demand for other long-haired fur such as fox and raccoon. If the skunk's luxurious, jet-black-and-white fur ever develops a following in North America, the skunk could become a major furbearer and there is no predicting what price the pelts might bring.

There are four separate species of skunks found in the United States: the spotted skunk, the striped skunk, the hog-nosed skunk, and the hooded skunk. For trapping purposes, all of these can be lumped into two categories: the spotted skunk, which is small, and the larger skunks, which include the hooded, hog-nosed, and striped.

The spotted skunk is commonly called the civet cat, polecat, smell cat, and plain old skunk. The pelt of the spotted skunk is of substantially greater value than the other, larger skunks despite the size because of the lesser amount of white; in fact, the less white on a skunk the better because the white yellows and does not take dye well. In Missouri, spotted skunks recently reached prices upwards of $11 per pelt. The spotted skunk rarely exceeds two and one half pounds, compared to the 10 to 12 pounds occasionally reached by the larger skunks. As with all skunks, the males run about 15 percent larger than females and the markings are the same in both sexes. The spotted skunk is unmistakable with its long, jet-black hair and white markings. The larger white marks are actually stripes with spots occurring in matched pairs on the back and sides of the tail.

The larger skunks are commonly called polecats, two stripers, double stripes, and smell cats; they are unmistakable. They are more widespread than the spotted skunk occurring in all sorts of habitat including suburbs and even the middle of large cities. Striped skunks are often seen as road kills having fallen victim, in turn, where they have come seeking road-kill carrion. They are extremely common in areas where substantial amounts of carrion are available; dumps and bodies of water where dead aquatic animals can be found fairly teem with striped skunks.

Both the spotted and larger striped skunks are omnivorous with an extremely broad diet consisting of plants and animals, and a very high percentage of insects including grasshoppers, crickets, and beetles. Other foods are rats, mice, salamanders, frogs, crayfish, fruit, corn, eggs (both wild and domestic), and a bit of poultry, but only as carrion. Skunks are a paradox for farmers. They could be viewed as beneficial since they reduce pests and have little if any impact on domestic fowl, yet their smell or their reputation makes them very unpopular with farmers. Skunks, interestingly enough, like to eat bees, which make them less than welcome to beekeepers.

Skunks, while widely distributed and adaptable to virtually any habitat, prefer semiopen country, mixed edges, returning fields, and farmland. The claws of the skunks are well adapted to digging both for food and for denning up, but the skunk appears to have a marked preference for abandoned dens of foxes or groundhogs; even stumps and old building foundations may harbor skunks.

The secret of the great numbers of skunks is simple reproductive prolificity. The striped skunks mate in late winter and give birth in approximately nine weeks to six or seven young. The young are weaned at 8 to 10 weeks so the field is full of adults each year. The spotted skunk ordinarily has a litter of only four or five, but the weaning is sooner and the young are adults in only three months.

Without question, the most distinctive feature about the skunk is the scent which is the primary defense system. This scent has its origin in twin nozzles located within the anal tract. The skunk is able to emit a stream of the vile musk with remarkable accuracy up to 10 feet and the scattergun effect will make up for any lack of pinpoint accuracy at ranges up to 30 feet. The musk is an oily, yellowish-white liquid with the active ingredient mercaptan, a sulphide. A splattering of this musk can be painful, can cause temporary blindness, and at the very least will make the unfortunate victim very unpopular for some time to come. No soap in existence can remove that scent quickly and thoroughly, and only avoiding the smell will assure the trapper of human companionship. The one encouraging aspect of that defense system is the skunk's reluctance to use it. The reluctance is surprising since skunks are sluggish and can only muster a top speed of about 10 miles per hour, climb poorly, and have poor senses of sight, smell, and hearing. Although a member of the weasel family, the skunk is not a good fighter and in fact is in all ways a retiring creature who would rather flee than fight and will ordinarily threaten before spraying even when cornered, perhaps sensing that the musk can only be used a few times before being exhausted.

So much for the accidental spraying, but the trapper must still cope with the problem of a skunk in a trap. Skunks taken by humane traps such as the conibear are seldom a problem. The scent is often released in a humane trap, but the smell is concentrated on the ground around the set. The animal can be pelted and the pelt dropped into a plastic bag which is tied off to control the scent until it can be aired and stretched prior to fleshing and drying. Disposable plastic gloves worn while pelting skunks can eliminate most or all of the scent transfer problem which can occur with skunks.

Skunks caught in a leghold or box trap can present still another problem. A skunk's reluctance to use its musk continues when trapped and protects the trapper until he gets very close. However, this is not the time for fancy tricks: reports have it that a skunk can spray even when held up by the tail. Obviously, this is no time to use a club. Just how to kill that skunk is a problem pondered by novice and old-timer alike with a noteworthy lack of consistent results. The real problem is how to cope with the scent which is usually released reflexively even after an instantaneous death. The solutions to this problem range from the serious to the tongue-in-cheek to the downright silly. Some trappers say that a bullet which severs the spinal cord will kill the animal without a spraying. Maybe, but how does one know with certainty how to hit that spinal cord? A brain shot will not do it. A box-trapped skunk can be drowned easily. Exhaust fumes from an automobile provide an effective, humane means of killing a skunk if an enclosed space is available to contain the skunk and fumes.

And then there are the suggestions that the trapper toss a plastic sheet over the animal and club everything that appears to be the skunk until the trapper is certain the skunk has been killed. Others suggest a head shot, leaving the animal in the trap overnight prior to returning for the pelt. One school of thought believes that a head shot will give the trapper seven seconds to remove the animal before the reflexive spraying. Another suggests shooting the animal in the head twice in order to get 14 seconds if the extra time is needed.

Pelting and stretching is covered elsewhere, but one comment on handling skunk pelts is necessary. When skinning the skunk, the anus will be isolated; many trappers tie the anus before pulling the pelt as this can eliminate any residual discharge of scent.

There are a couple of final words necessary on skunk scent. First, while nothing known to man will remove that smell quickly and thoroughly, tomato juice will dampen it more quickly than anything else and leave only faint effluvia to fade with time. Finally, skunk scent does not necessarily ruin a set or trap. There is, in fact, good evidence that the scent actually attracts other skunks and curious animals. A good dash of skunk scent may be the best thing that can happen to a live trap.

MUSKRAT

Of all the furbearers in North America, the muskrat might seem to be the least likely candidate to be the leading furbearer, but it is. Even the name is derogatory; literally reduced to its components, muskrat means "strong smelling rodent." No other furbearer even approaches the numbers of muskrat taken each year and, with the demand for natural fur continuing on the rise, the dollar value of the muskrat pelt may exceed that of all other furbearers combined.

Muskrats are another of those animals that people tend to be ambivalent about. They are attractive to observe and the pelts are of

North America's number one furbearer: the muskrat.
(courtesy J.E. Osman and the Pennsylvania Game
Commission)

substantial value, but they also burrow through pond dams and irrigation canal walls thereby causing great damage.

Muskrats will usually reach two feet in length including the tail which is bald, scaly, and flattened vertically; a typical weight will be two and one half to three pounds. A muskrat might be mistaken for a small beaver except for the great differences in the tail. When prime, the muskrat's coat will be dull brown to black and composed of a soft, dense undercoat with a good quantity of longer guard hairs.

Prime muskrat habitat is swamp, marsh, or slow-moving streams with abundant aquatic plants, especially cattails and water lilies. Muskrats are largely vegetarian and will raid for grain, fruit, and garden crops if they are very close to water. The small percentage of animal matter muskrats eat consists of crawfish, mussels, fish, and frogs, plus carrion, including muskrat carrion. Muskrats do not hibernate. An interesting thing about muskrats is that their major predators — other than trappers — are mink which will often substantially reduce the numbers of muskrats to be found in a confined area.

Muskrats are often cited as an animal that needs to be trapped for its own good or at least for the good of the marsh. This is because the muskrat is a prolific breeder and, even more, a voracious eater. When a population peak hits the muskrat marsh, muskrats will eat everything their teeth will sink into, including each other. Those feeding binges often see the marsh denuded of vegetation and the muskrats eating their own dens. A population drop from starvation, exposure, and related diseases is inevitable.

Muskrat pelts are of considerable but not great value and the species' position as a major furbearer is largely based upon the enormous numbers which are trapped annually. This large harvest is possible only because muskrats are prolific breeders. Females may have two, three, or even four litters in a season with the average litter numbering six.

Some muskrat trappers use as many as 500 traps and expect at times to harvest one muskrat per trap per day. Some special ideas may be helpful in putting a muskrat in all — or at least most — traps.

One extraordinarily successful technique for muskrat trapping takes advantage of the rodent's tendency to climb or swim between obstructions to get to something. For example, muskrats will swim to a bank and climb out between two sticks in the water rather than choose a clear spot. This could be due to the muskrat's desire to have something to grasp or scramble up on. Whatever the reason, a trapper can take advantage of that trait when setting traps. A scooped-out notch on a bank near food plots or lodges will result in good catches. Another approach is to add a couple of guide sticks around the trap but lodged in the bank to invite the muskrat in. A baited floating vegetation trap high on both sides and with a low watery spot in the middle will entice about every muskrat that sees it.

The famous floating set elsewhere described is remarkably productive for muskrat trappers primarily where there is no other sitting place available. In addition, the trapper can improve his catch on a floating set by putting some sort of a cover, however crude, over the floating set. Of course, a floating set should fairly bristle with traps as any number of muskrats might use the floating set during a short period of time.

If one direct statement could be made about muskrat trapping, it is that there is no need to hide traps. Of course, most muskrat sets will be water sets, but it is reassuring to know that there is no need to bury the traps. However, one point does need to be remembered — every effort should be made to make the trap accessible to the muskrat and easily sprung if the animal does step into it. This means that the jaws should

Prime muskrats

be level and the pan either level with the jaws or slightly below. Further, the trap should be on a line where the muskrat will easily make contact without being obliged to step up into the trap. Neither should the muskrat cross over a jaw at right angles; the animal should cross the hinge, not the jaw.

Since the muskrat leghold set can be made without any cover, one problem may be keeping floating debris from drifting or being accidentally pushed into the trap by swimming muskrats. The potentially troublesome materials in the area should be cleared away and the guide stakes may help control the litter also.

75

A long-spring leghold trap should be set to anticipate the approach of the muskrat and to avoid a loss from the trap throwing the animal's leg free from the grip of the jaws. This means that in addition to bringing up the jaws to close parallel with the approach, the trapper must also place the spring away from possible approach and around far enough to let the loose jaw lie flat and thereby open as far as possible.

The use of the term "killer set" is almost meaningless with muskrats because the relentless assault a trapped muskrat makes on a leghold trap necessitates a drowning set or there will almost certainly be a wring-off which is unspeakably cruel and a total loss to all involved.

Run sets made with the conibear trap are perhaps the most productive of all muskrat sets. Runs are easily located in calm water as they are clearly discernible on the bottom. The conibear is set in such a way as to anticipate the approach of the muskrat. As the accompanying illustrations in the sets section indicate, the use of guide stakes to make the conibear opening the most attractive route to take is strongly advised.

The drowning set will be the mainstay of the trapper who prefers to use a leghold. The accompanying illustration in the sets section indicates several potential leghold sets which could be used in conjunction with a drowning set for muskrats.

Probably the best-known muskrat trapping advance in decades is the "stop loss" or "sure grip" leghold trap which is now widely available. The stop loss has an extra bail which acts like a third trap jaw and is released after the other two jaws have been closed. The bail snaps down with a force that often kills the animal outright. Muskrats that survive the initial blow are frequently held low enough to drown even in shallow water and are virtually always pinned down to the point that they cannot wiggle and flop about to wring off. The stop loss also eliminates the otherwise great need to catch the muskrat by the hind leg. Consistently catching muskrats by the hind leg requires a real measure of skill. The trap must be set in such a way as to permit the animal to pass over with the front feet and yet step onto it with the rear leg. This can be done regularly by keeping the trap at muskrat landings and placing the trap very close to the step-off point. However, the most skillful sets with conventional traps will sometimes have muskrats pass completely over, sometimes catch them by the front leg and, worst of all, will sometimes allow wring-off.

Due to their semiaquatic nature and great concentrations, muskrats lend themselves to a type of trap which may capture several animals at one setting. The colony trap, also referred to as a basket trap or cage trap, is of wire-frame construction with one-way, swinging doors at each end. As much as five feet long, the colony trap is to be set in a well-traveled run with guide stakes to funnel the muskrats in. Once inside the colony trap, the muskrats cannot escape and, since the set is underwater, the animals expire in a short time. Some jurisdictions do not permit the use of the colony trap, presumably because of the danger of overharvest.

MINK

Trends in fashion fluctuate, but the mink seems to remain the class animal of the furbearer field. This small member of the weasel family has been subject to such demand that an entire ranching industry complete with its own magazines and specialized markets grew up around it. The fluctuation of the markets ended a great number of those ranches in less than ideal financial circumstances, but the restrengthening of the market for all natural furs is renewing faith in the industry. The market for the wild pelts has never looked better. Prices have been very good, reaching an average of over $18 in 1978 and well over $22 in 1981.

Mink are semiaquatic members of the weasel family. This highly sought furbearer will measure about two feet in length, about one third of that being tail, and will weigh up to three pounds; female mink run significantly smaller than males. The mink is physically very much like a weasel with short legs, short head, pointed muzzle, and a serpentine, long, bushy tail. The pelt is lustrous with long guard hairs over a dense underfur. Mink do not turn white like their other cousin weasels called ermine, but the colors range from russet to a rich dark brown.

As furbearers go, the mink has excellent hearing and sight as well as sense of smell. Mink are mostly nocturnal with activity confined to water for great periods followed by days of careful, loping exploration of the land. Mink are among the most curious of all animals and while traveling will explore every nook, cranny, and crevice of its habitat. The range for a male mink is fairly large — one to three miles average with females traveling much less.

Like most members of the weasel family, the mink is a consummate predator and can handle prey substantially larger than itself. Favorite foods of the mink include muskrats, mice and other rodents, shrews, fish, frogs, crayfish, insects, and bird eggs. Mink are more or less opportunistic feeders and will take whatever they can get easily. They

Mink

are the foremost wild predator of muskrats; a mink will occasionally kill far more than it can eat and store the surplus.

Mink den in logs, exposed roots, groundhog holes, and vacant muskrat lodges which they often *make* vacant. The sole requirement is proximity to water. Mink line their dens with grass, leaves, and fur. A mink will commonly have several dens over its range. Mink are basically solitary animals except during mating season, which is from February to April and peaks in March. Delivery of the litter is ordinarily in May and typically consists of two to seven extremely small animals. The average litter is four. Young mink develop quickly and disperse by fall having reached sexual maturity by the age of approximately 10 months. Mink are preyed on by fox, great horned owls, bobcats, and, of course, trappers.

Mink are treated by some trappers, especially beginning trappers, with a reverence that approaches mysticism. Listening to some conversations concerning mink trapping would lead to the conclusion that mink are elusive will-of-the-wisps possessing both a supernatural ability to avoid traps and an intelligence superior to that of the average trapper. In fact, mink are not much more difficult to trap than other semiaquatic animals, but there simply are not as many mink as, for example, muskrats. And everyone is after the few mink that are available. There are approximately one million mink trapped in North America each year and there is a great deal of real estate surrounding each of those mink. A lone male mink may not pass by a given spot for a week or more but, if no predator or trapper gets that mink, it will eventually come by the same spot.

Other than the basic blind sets on dry land or water, or better still, a combination of both, there are two specialties for mink trapping. First, there is a so-called bridge set which relies on the fact that mink have an observed peculiarity for going around culvert underpasses rather than through them. No. 1½ legholds in drowning sets placed at the sides of a stream bridge will take fair numbers of mink if there are any to be had. Muskrats and raccoon will blunder into the same set. Second, owing to the mink's invariable habit of exploring every trickle of water coming into the stream or marsh, traps should be set in a blind set at the confluence of any such trickle of water. These so-called mink streams may be nothing more than small fresh water runoffs, yet a blind set will take mink wading up in search of whatever interests them. Other sets for mink are discussed and illustrated in detail in the other sections.

OTTER

Otter pelts are the most durable of all natural furs. The pelt is a beautiful rich brown with a lighter underside. Consequently, the otter commands a very good price and the pelt is highly prized. However, the otter is a major furbearer because of the high price, not as the result of a large harvest. Otters are members of the weasel family and are good hunters that prefer to kill their own prey. Favorite foods of this semiaquatic furbearer include fish, minnows, frogs, snails, mussels, insects, the occasional aquatic plant, and even muskrats. The otter is a large animal, two and one half to three and one half feet in length plus tail; weights of 15 to 25 pounds are about normal with the female running smaller than the male.

The most durable of all natural furs comes from the otter.

Otters are extremely wary animals with excellent hearing and eyesight. The sense of smell is also well developed. The most skillful swimmer among land mammals, the otter can swim fast, dive to depths of 50 feet and remain submerged for five minutes or even a bit longer; otters often travel downstream as far as one quarter mile underwater.

The otter has a reputation of being an almost unbelievably elusive quarry for the trapper. The difficulty probably stems from the fact that there simply are not very many otters even in good habitat. Many jurisdictions have responded to this by closing or severely limiting the trapping season on otters. Otters do not have their first litter until age three and the litters are small, usually numbering two or three.

Otters require clear water with good populations of fish and other aquatic life to thrive. Pollution of streams and other encroachments by man upon the environment have reduced the otter numbers. The most likely spots for otter trapping are areas with many small streams and pools. Otters seem to like beaver dams and dislike mink, which they will kill, although not for food.

Otters are extremely powerful animals and the likelihood of taking one accidentally in a mink or raccoon set is remote as the otter will twist free. Some otters are taken annually in beaver sets, however. A large leghold (No. 4 double long-spring, preferably) or a No. 330 conibear is the choice for otter trapping.

An interesting thing about the otter is the difficulty in skinning it. The otter is not so much skinned as it has its pelt cut, inch by inch, from the carcass. In this sense, the otter is somewhat like the beaver except that otters are case pelted.

The otter sets are adaptations of the basic blind sets and runway sets. A large percentage of otter taken are captured in sets intended for beaver. Despite the excellent price otter pelts bring, the animal's scarcity limits the number of trappers actively seeking them.

MARTEN

The marten is a member of the weasel family, approximately the size of a mink but with longer fur, larger eyes, and more prominent ears. A marten, also known as the American Sable because of its resemblance to the Russian Sable, is a tree climber with agility equaling that of a squirrel.

The marten (courtesy Mark Brown)

The marten is a non-fussy, opportunistic eater who will consume insects, fruits, eggs, squirrels, and other small mammals. Marten dens are hollow trees where litters of three to five young are born in the spring.

Marten are no longer common in their former range that once stretched throughout all of the Northern United States and Canada. The range now is primarily Canada and Alaska plus parts of the Pacific Northwest, the Rockies, and a few places in the Northeastern United States. The range reduction is a result of land-use abuses; the marten is adaptable but not to the point of surviving over-logging and unregulated trapping. Trapping marten is confined to areas with substantial populations which basically means the northern regions of the United States and on into Canada. Climate there being what it is, the marten trapper must be accustomed to some fairly rigorous conditions. The weather conditions dictate some extra precautions to keep the traps in working order. Fortunately, the marten is not trap shy and can be taken in a baited trap right out in the open. Most marten sets are placed high, well above the snow level, and the trap itself is well lubricated, preferably with a vinyl coating of Teflon so the temperature extremes will not have any effect.

Marten pelts bring an extremely high price. The pelts are another of those that should be presented fur side out. After stretching and fleshing, the marten pelt is left overnight in a normal state and then reversed on the board while still flexible.

COYOTE

The sudden interest in long-haired fur has driven the prices of coyote pelts to incredible levels. This turn of events is more surprising when the recent absence of demand for the coyote pelt is considered. From the late 1940s to the mid-1960s, coyote pelts never approached one dollar and periodically dropped as low as 20 cents.

The coyote may be another example of what anthropomorphism — giving human traits to nonhumans — can do. The coyote has been variously described in the media as sneaky, mangy, conniving, and, in the very popular Road Runner cartoons, downright stupid. None of this aided the public image of the coyote, but the demand for the fur has now become very respectable.

In fact, the coyote is a very wary and extremely intelligent quarry. It has been suggested that, given the coyote's ability to adapt to a changing environment and to thrive where other animals fail, the coyote may be the last animal to survive at the end of time. Presumably, the coyote will be using the last traces of human endeavor as a scent post.

The coyote's size is sort of a compromise; larger than a fox but smaller than a wolf. The superficial resemblance between a coyote and a small wolf is striking and many people refer to the coyote as a brush wolf. An adult coyote will weigh 20 to 35 pounds with the exceptional specimen going 40 pounds. The Eastern version of coyote, however, runs considerably larger and occasionally reaches 50 pounds or more. Speculation is that they are larger because they are interbred with domestic animals.

Coyotes breed in the dead of winter, January and February, and deliver a litter of 4 to 12 in late March through April. Young coyotes grow extremely fast and by late fall to early winter are almost indistinguishable from adults. The preferred range is along permanent water with dense undergrowth except in the American Southwest where

Coyote—also known as brush wolf or red wolf. (courtesy Jay Kaffka)

open country harbors coyotes. Coyotes are capable of digging but prefer to take cover as they find it: old badger holes, small caves, and natural crevices are prime choices. Coyotes are opportunistic feeders — they eat what is available — and are basically carnivorous with a preference for small rodents such as mice and cottontails. However, they will threaten larger animals including domestic animals and even their cousin, the fox. The small bit of vegetable matter that the coyote will eat is not sufficient to make it a potential bait. Studies indicate that coyotes have virtually no impact on the deer herd but feed on them almost exclusively as carrion.

The cautiousness of coyotes (and foxes) is almost legendary. This has resulted in all sorts of elaborate, esoteric sets being created. One set, described in a publication of the South Dakota Department of Game, Fish and Parks, deserves verbatim presentation here:

The gang set is made in a barren area of at least seventy-five square yards. It must be perfectly level, devoid of vegetation, windswept, and with good visibility in all directions. In the approximate center a carcass of a large animal is staked down solidly. The carcass may be a badger, coon, beaver or even a "skun out" fox. With the claw hammer we rake up loose earth evenly in a four foot diameter all around or over the carcass. We then finish the job of covering, with a scratch tool, to obliterate claw hammer marks and to simulate animal claw marks. Fox urine is then sprinkled lightly over the finished job. Then at approximate distances of about seventy-five feet from the carcass we set four traps, one each at NW, NE, SE, and SW directions from the carcass. At each set we rake up an egg-shaped mound, roughly, about four inches high and about six inches wide. The slightly tapered point of the mound should point toward the carcass. In the end of this point we plant a small cow chip, on edge and at a slight angle leaning away from the trap which is set with the pan from five to nine inches away from the chip. A bit of call lure is dropped on the base of the cow chip and fox urine is sprinkled lightly over the completed set. The same general procedure is repeated at each of the other three sets only we use a different lure at each one, perhaps omitting lure at one using just urine. Different objects may be used in the mounds at each set. Small bones, magpie or crow wings, or small plants could be used. These are all scratch-type sets, as applied in a gang set. A few claw marks can be made around each set with the scratch tool although it should not be overdone. It is also called a square set — with four traps — or a triangle set with three traps. Any or all versions of it can be made in such areas as burned out straw stacks, or short grazed grass in summer pastures and in our region, in the barren slack areas of abandoned coal mines.

In fact, the basic scent-post set, dirt-hole set, and carcass set will take coyote wherever there are coyotes to be taken. The trapper needs to remember that coyotes are intelligent and roam over great areas, taking their food as they find it. They follow regular trails and frequent the same crossings. When they roam, they take the path of least resistance — they walk where the going is easiest. Coyotes like to find high ground and look over the area. The pathways are dotted with scent posts where they urinate regularly. They have acute senses of sight, hearing, and smell. With these facts in mind, a trapper can locate and capture coyotes if the animals are present.

BADGER

The badger is a giant member of the weasel family ranging in size up to three feet in length and weighing 15 to 25 pounds. Like most of its other weasel cousins, the badger is possessed of a fierce disposition and voracious appetite that can be satisfied only with fresh meat. Since the badger feeds almost exclusively on rodents, it might ordinarily be seen as an ally to the landowner. However, since the badger digs for its prey, it leaves all sorts of holes and ruts, which make it about as welcome as a groundhog. Because the badger is a nuisance to landowners and especially to those with livestock, it is often possible to get permission to trap these animals on private land.

The badger

Badgers give birth to small litters, from two to five young is typical, in late March or early April. Their dens are no more distinctive at first glance than a groundhog hole but in fact tend to be larger and oval shaped. They inhabit mostly open, prairie-type areas but also are found in returning borders.

Until recently, the badger pelt has not been particularly prized, but was a somewhat dubious bonus catch for fox trappers. The pelts did not command high or even respectable prices since they were almost a novelty. With the renewed interest in wild trapped pelts, however, the badger has become a real prize, with the pelt's price rivaling fox and coyote and actually exceeding that of raccoon.

Badgers are taken in the standard dirt-hole and bank-hole sets. While these sets are covered elsewhere, one special note should be made here. Badgers are large, heavy animals with wide-set feet, bowed legs, and an abdomen that touches the ground. Trappers making sets that may attract the canine furbearers or badger should have two traps closely placed, as the badger may walk right over a single trap, straddling it with those wide-set feet.

Badgers are the only major furbearer, other than beavers, that are not routinely case skinned. Badgers are open skinned and stretched flat as square as possible.

A final word about badgers: the term "badgering" implies a sort of relentless blood-thirsty pursuit. The term is appropriate for the badger, which is a fierce, courageous fighter and is a tough customer when trapped. The trapped badger should be treated with the utmost respect.

BOBCAT

The bobcat is easily the more common of the two feline furbearers. Averaging about 36 inches long, including the stub of the tail from which it takes its name, a bobcat generally weighs 18 to 22 pounds although it may occasionally reach 35 pounds or a bit more. There are two other distinctive features of the bobcat. One is the large tufts of fur that extend out and downward from the ears. The other is that the length of the back leg exceeds that of the front leg. The unusual leg length difference results in a peculiar, sloping running gait.

Bobcats breed early in March, giving birth to small litters of two to five young in mid-May. The den may be a small cave, rock crevice, or even a hollow log. The young are weaned at two months and remain

Young bobcats are sometimes not much larger than a big housecat. (courtesy Jacqueline Geary)

with the mother through most of the first year. They are not fast growing animals and seldom weigh more than 12 to 15 pounds at the age of one year.

Bobcats cannot tolerate people and prefer territory that is as wild as possible. They prefer dense undergrowth or secondary growth similar to that which harbors deer. However, studies indicate that bobcats have very little impact on a deer herd, because the relatively small predator has contact with only very sick or dead animals the size of a deer. The staples of the bobcat diet are rodents and other small mammals, although it is an opportunistic feeder that will take an occasional mink, shrew, fish, frog, insect, or even porcupine or fox. The bobcat is extremely wary and is considered by many trappers to be the most elusive of all furbearers. The senses of sight and smell are keen and hearing is extraordinarily acute.

The bobcat pelt has enjoyed some measure of popularity for several years, but resurgence of interest in natural furs has been especially favorable for the bobcat trapper. The increased trapping and hunting of

The pelting process begins on a small bobcat. (courtesy Jacqueline Geary)

this animal, which suddenly has the most valuable pelt of the more common furbearers, has led to cutbacks or complete elimination of a bobcat season in many jurisdictions. The bobcat is not all that numerous in most parts of North America. The bobcat is common only in the arid parts of the American Southwest. There and in the densely covered lowlands farther north, the bobcat ranges over a remarkably large territory. A trap set in an excellent location may be untouched for a week or more simply because the territory of the bobcat is so large that it will not pass by very often. However, the bobcat is a creature of habit with well-established routes. Careful scouting and patience are necessary for a harvest of bobcats.

Where trapping is allowed, the bobcat is most often taken with dirt-hole sets, trail sets, and carcass sets. Bobcats pursue their quarry by use of both scent and sight, so skilled trappers often use some version of a wing set to attract the eye.

RACCOON

The raccoon is the second most valuable wild trapped furbearer in North America. In many areas and even in entire states, it is the leader in dollar value if not in numbers taken. The recent fashion trend favoring long-haired fur has pushed the price of raccoon pelts to record levels previously undreamed of, rivaling the inflated prices mink and muskrat brought at the end of World War I. Some softening of the demand for long fur plus the mild winter and the related record harvest in the 1979-80 season eased the prices back down somewhat, but the raccoon pelt was, and still is, a real prize.

The raccoon is most often viewed with ambivalence. Raccoon, especially those living near civilization, can be very destructive to crops and positively devastating to both wild and domestic birds. The same raccoon can be extremely valuable as furbearers with some prices reaching and even exceeding $60. Raccoon flesh is considered a delicacy by many. Finally, raccoon hunting with dogs as a sport has a long, colorful history, a very devoted following and at least one magazine solely dedicated to it; *Full Cry* is a monthly magazine with raccoon hunting as its only topic.

Adult raccoon are from 30 to 40 inches in length including the tail and weigh from 10 to 30 pounds with males generally larger than females. Reports of extremely large raccoon weighing 40 pounds or more

90

The second-most valuable furbearer — the raccoon. (courtesy Mark Brown)

have been authenticated, but they are clearly not typical specimens. The raccoon can be found nearly anywhere but appears most frequently around permanent water. The raccoon is neither aquatic nor semi-aquatic but finds hunting and foraging along and in water very convenient. The well-known habit of raccoon "washing" food remains something of a mystery to naturalists although it is generally assumed that fastidiousness is not the reason but that an absence of salivary glands requires wetting of food or that the wetting permits a more accurate evaluation of the edible qualities of the food. Whatever the reason, trappers can take good advantage of the raccoon's reliance upon a water supply in choosing trap sites.

Raccoon may possess the keenest senses of sight, hearing, and smell of any furbearers. The sense of touch is also highly developed and permits them to catch minnows and other small fish. The animal is largely nocturnal and has excellent night vision.

A very large, prime raccoon. (courtesy Jacqueline Geary)

Raccoon are omnivorous — they eat anything. Included among the favorites are fruits — such as wild grapes and cherries, persimmons, apples, nuts and acorns, and melons. They also enjoy carrion, eggs, insects, fish, greens, frogs, and small mammals such as mice. Corn is a special favorite; a few raccoon foraging through a stand of sweet corn can ruin it in a single night.

Concentrations of raccoon, depending on food supply and habitat, can be very high. Some studies indicate that excellent raccoon habitat may harbor one or more per acre although habitat rated as merely good might require two acres to support one raccoon. The raccoon breeds early in the year and produces a litter of three to five young in April. The young are weaned in four months, although there tends to be some "family" grouping on through the winter.

While raccoon seem able to adapt and thrive anywhere, including suburbs and even in cities, the best raccoon habitat is varied. Trees of various sizes and species with lots of low cover are preferred, especially if permanent water is available. While foraging takes place almost exclusively on the ground, large den trees are helpful if not absolutely necessary. Swampy lands or farm hollows are good raccoon habitat.

Trapping raccoon tends to be best during the early season, because they load up on food early in the fall and, while they do not actually hibernate, their activities become very much reduced as temperatures drop below 25 degrees Fahrenheit.

BEAVER

If an animal could be given credit for opening up the interior of an entire continent, that animal could only be the *Castor canadensis*, better known as the beaver. In the early 1800s, a time when 50 to 75 cents per day was typical for a working man, beaver pelts brought the staggering sum of four dollars each. Uncontrolled trapping and hunting for the enormous rodent severely eroded the population, but fashion reversed the trend in time to save the beaver. Now, due to prolific breeding, the beaver has been restored to most of its former ranges and in many places is actually becoming something of a pest. The recent increase in trapping interest has led at least one state — Missouri — to shorten the trapping season except on beaver for which a more liberal season has been established. Beavers do not hibernate as such, therefore, the longer seasons now available in certain jurisdictions can be used by trappers who may be forced to take the animals through ice.

The beaver is another furbearer that is met with ambivalence. It is an undeniably beautiful animal and fascinating for its engineering ability. However, that engineering skill means a loss of at least some timber and eventually leads to flooding of dammed-up streams. As a fur animal, the beaver is currently in a peculiar position. The beaver pelt is of excellent quality and is extremely durable. However, while the price of the large pelts has been improving, it is still relatively low.

People not familiar with beavers tend to be startled at the dimensions of these furbearers. The adult beaver will weigh around 35 pounds

The beaver: nature's engineer. (courtesy J.E. Osman and the
Pennsylvania Game Commission)

and may be three to four and one-half feet in length, including the
distinctive flat, scaly tail which will often exceed one foot in length.
Fifty- to 60- pound specimens are not uncommon and animals up to 100
pounds have been reported by reliable sources. The size of beaver pelts is
also impressive. Measurements of the stretched pelts are made from the
eyes to the tail and then across the widest part. The two measurements
are added to give the size, which is grouped as follows: XX Large, over 65
inches; X Large, over 60 inches; Large, over 55 inches; Large Medium,
over 52 inches; Medium, over 48 inches; Small, over 45 inches; and Kit,
under 45 inches.

Beavers have remarkable dexterity in their "hands" when working

94

on dams, digging, and manipulating bits of food. They do not possess good vision but their senses of hearing and smell are excellent. Beavers remain very close to water or in the water as they are very slow moving on dry land but very mobile in water.

The beaver is strictly a vegetarian with a preference for soft vegetable foods such as grass, mushrooms, and cattails. They also will fell trees for food with the preference being aspen, maple, willow, beech, and wild cherry. The continuous growing of the prominent front teeth of a beaver necessitates a constant gnawing to keep the growth in check. This accounts for the famed industriousness of beavers. Larger trees are felled in order to reach the more succulent upper reaches. The parts of the tree which are not consumed are cut into smaller pieces and used to build dams. While the beaver rarely ventures too far from water, it may go upwards of 200 yards onto dry land to fell a tree. The engineering of beavers often involves digging canals to float a fallen tree to a pond. The beaver's activity of damming and the resultant flooding will lead to an exhaustion of an area for beaver inhabitation within about 10 years after which the beavers will be forced to move on.

Longer seasons on beaver sometimes mean trapping through ice. (courtesy Mark Brown)

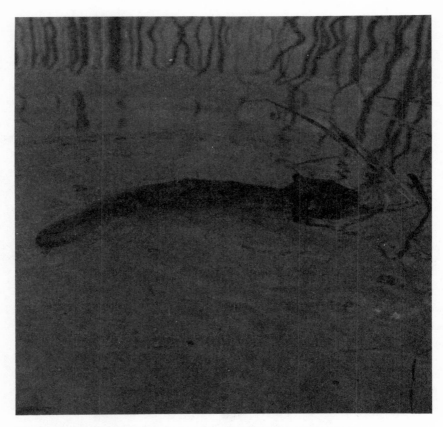

The beaver is more at home in water than on land. (courtesy
J.E. Osman and the Pennsylvania Game Commission)

Beaver lodges are unmistakable, large domed islands of logs and
mud. The beaver's litter of kits, usually numbering four or five, are
delivered in the lodge in April or May. A lodge often harbors three
generations of beavers at a time as beavers do not mature until age two.
This type of lodge is called a beaver colony.

The very size and vitality of beavers make trapping difficult. The
relentless struggle against a trap by a muskrat is well known; the beaver
duplicates the effort and it is 10 to 20 times the size of the muskrat. The
only reasonable way to trap beaver is with a drowning set and even this
is difficult since a beaver can stay under water for 15 minutes without
drawing a breath. Humane traps like the No. 330 conibear set in underwater runs or at the den are the best bet.

The beaver is one of the furbearers with all sorts of valuable parts. The pelt, of course, is valuable. The scent glands of the beaver are called castors and are located on the underside of the hind leg; these castors can be made into scent or lure devices and used to manufacture perfume so they should not be discarded. Finally, the meat of beaver is excellent table fare as it is a rich meat which bears a strong resemblance to roast beef. For this reason, a trapper should be reluctant to sell a beaver with the fur on or "in the round" although, as will be explained later, the beaver is without question the most difficult animal to pelt.

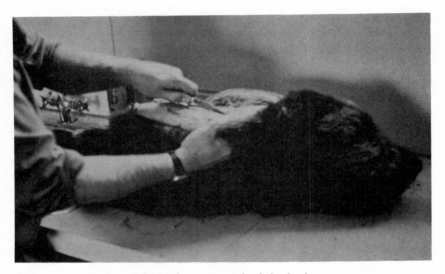

The beaver pelt is cut from the carcass inch by inch.
(courtesy Mark Brown)

NUTRIA

The nutria is a South American transplant, apparently having arrived in the United States in the late 1930s. These animals have a relatively limited range in the United States. Large populations are confined roughly to the Gulf Coastal region, areas with warm marsh areas, the states of North Carolina and Maryland, and the maritime climate areas of Oregon and Washington state. However, where nutria do occur, they tend to dominate because of their physical characteristics.

The nutria (courtesy Jay Kaffka)

First, the nutria prefers habitat very much like that favored by the muskrat: swamps and marshes, lakes, streams, and backwaters. Nutria burrow out dens in levees and shorelines; they feed and rest on above-water platforms that they build out of vegetation. Nutria are almost exclusively vegetarians, preferring grass, cattails, and duckweed, although they occasionally will eat willows when the water conditions dictate.

Second, the nutria will weigh from 12 to 17½ pounds at maturity — a very impressive size compared to a muskrat, which will run two to three pounds. Nutria have an enmity for muskrats and reports have authenticated nutria killing and eating the smaller rodents. The nutria's size and food preferences serve to reduce the number of muskrats in a given area quickly once the nutria gets a hold.

Actually, the nutria and muskrat bear a strong, if superficial, resemblance; the nutria looks like a large, economy-sized muskrat except that its tail is round and not flattened vertically. Similar to the muskrat and all other rodents, the nutria is a prolific breeder that reaches sexual maturity less than one year from its birth. Litters usually number four or five young and it is not uncommon for a female to have five litters in two years. The young are usually weaned at five to seven weeks, after which the parents have nothing to do with the offspring. A unique feature of the nutria is that the female's feeders are located along the sides of the back and, as a result, the animal can nurse its young while swimming.

The nutria's place in the fur industry is interesting. Probably because of the limited range, very little is heard about the nutria in trapping publications that are forever discussing muskrats. Even when reference is made to the state of Louisiana, the first mention is of the enormous muskrat harvest when, in fact, the numbers and values of nutria harvested in Louisiana far exceed those for muskrats. Nutria are considered pests because they damage crops and compete with other wildlife. Totally unprotected for years, nutria are now within the trapping codes and they have a very respectable market.

Nutria trapping is a compromise between muskrat trapping and beaver trapping because the nutria has the muskrat's relentless vitality on the one hand and the beaver's size on the other. Trappers who take nutria consistently use essentially the same techniques as for beaver or muskrat with allowances for size. The lures used for beaver and muskrats will work very well on nutria, also.

FOX — RED AND GRAY

Foxes also are numbered among the animals that have been especially affected by the renewed interest in long-haired fur. From the late 1940s to the 1960s, the price of fox rarely approached one dollar for the average pelt. Pelt prices in recent years, however, have been so high that numerous jurisdictions have closed the season on fox except in very

Red fox

exceptional circumstances such as no kill running with dogs.

There are very significant physical differences between the two species. Red foxes average 22 to 25 inches in length excluding a 14- to 16-inch tail; they weigh 8 to 12 pounds. Gray foxes are usually smaller with a size running from 21 to 29 inches excluding an 11- to 16-inch tail; grays will weigh approximately 7 to 13 pounds. One universal mistake about foxes is overestimating their weight, a common error probably due to their full, thick fur which makes them appear much larger than they actually are. Red foxes have unmistakable, reddish-orange fur, black ears, legs, and feet; the tail is relatively long and bushy with a white tip. The gray is really more black and gray with coarser hair than the red; the underfur is cream colored. The bushy tail of the gray is tipped black rather than white. The track of the two species can be distinguished readily; the gray has much larger toe pads but a smaller foot overall than the red.

There are very broad color ranges within the red fox species, some occurring frequently. The so-called cross fox is a red fox with dark fur running down the back and across the shoulders forming a cross. The silver fox is a variation of the red fox with hair actually being black, although the longer guard hairs show up as white, thus resulting in a frosted look. These variations are always red foxes with the one common identifying characteristic being the white-tipped tail.

Foxes breed in February and usually give birth in late April or early May to six kits, although the litter may number as high as 10. The young are born in dens — the famous fox hole — that are ordinarily enlarged groundholes, small rock crevices, or simply hollowed-out logs. The kits are weaned in two to three months and leave the parents before fall.

Both red and gray foxes are opportunistic feeders with preferences for small animals, among them rodents, possums, and birds, as well as fruit. Their scavenging accounts for frequent sightings at roadsides and the relatively high number of foxes that become road kills despite their intelligence.

Habitat preferences for reds and grays are not the same. Reds prefer sparsely settled areas with woods and permanent water. The red fox also seems less concerned with people, often living in areas with heavily traveled roads. Red foxes sometimes thrive literally within a city and there are occasional Sunday supplement-type articles about suburbanites with foxes in their backyards. Gray foxes are less compatible with human contact and therefore prefer dense forest cover. Where the two species overlap, the more aggressive gray tends to dominate.

The reproductive capacity of foxes is not all that high, but they have no wild predators to speak of, although the large wild feline and coyote will occasionally take a fox. Consequently, population swings are fairly common. Excellent fox habitat might harbor 12 or more foxes per square mile with the average run being less than one quarter of that number.

Most foxes trapped each year are young animals on the move and staking out a territory. Because of this, the scent post is an especially effective set. The same sets are used for red and gray fox although far more gray fox catches are reported. The scent-post set, dirt-hole set, mound set, and campfire set will all take their share of foxes.

While care of pelts is considered elsewhere, a comment on stretching fox pelts is necessary here. Fox is one of the few pelts that is cured hide side in. The pelt first is stretched for a day hide side out, then, while still pliable, reversed and allowed to cure.

Gray foxes (courtesy J.E. Osman and the Pennsylvania Game Commission)

Canada lynx—the larger of the feline furbearers.

LYNX

The lynx is the larger of the common feline furbearers and occasionally reaches a weight of 50 pounds. The lynx prefers territory very similar to that of bobcats — dense, very sparsely populated forest land — and is almost totally incompatible with human beings. The lynx is not found in the southern portion of the bobcat range and it is so often associated with the northern part of the range it is very commonly termed the Canada lynx.

The lynx is not as opportunistic a feeder as the bobcat and subsists largely on rabbits, although it will attempt to kill a porcupine or take other rodents as the situation requires. Where the cycle of rabbit population drops due to disease, extreme cold, etc., the lynx population drops proportionately.

The recent resurgence of interest in wild furs has driven the lynx pelt prices to astronomical levels and trapping pressure is intense where the lynx is found. Sets that take bobcats will take lynx as well.

FISHER

The fisher is another tree-dwelling member of the weasel family. Its dark brown coat with lighter guard hairs gives it a frosted appearance. It bears a remarkable resemblance to the marten although it is substantially larger, sometimes reaching 40 inches in length including a 12- to 15-inch tail, and occasionally weighing as much as 15 pounds; female fisher are ordinarily no more than one half the size of males. The resemblance between fisher and marten is so great that casual observers can distinguish a small fisher from an adult marten only by the marten's buff throat patch. The fisher is opportunistic in nature and feeds upon rodents, birds, large carrion, and, a most unusual choice of fare, porcupine. The fisher is very skilled at rolling a porcupine over on its back to expose the soft underside and eats all but the quills.

Fisher are not prolific breeders, giving birth only once per year, in March or April, to a small litter numbering one to five. The gestation period of fisher is 338 to 358 days, with delayed implantation accounting for some of this. The fisher litter is born in a typical fisher den, ordinarily a cavity in a large tree or a rock crevice. Similar to the mink, the fisher may have several dens in a territory. Fisher young ordinarily stay with the mother for most of the first year.

Fisher require extensive forests for habitats and are not too well adapted to contact with man. They are actually relatively rare furbearers. A few northern areas of the United States, notably New York and Maine, have fisher populations that can be trapped. All Canadian provinces have fisher in their vast expanses of forests, but even where the population of fisher is relatively strong, the numbers are still low. There is evidence that over trapping can severely damage or even eliminate the fisher population. As a result, the fisher, where trapping is permitted, is protected by trapping codes.

The fisher pelt is one of the extremely valuable furbearer pelts and therefore is vigorously sought despite the scarcity of animals. The sets used for marten will work equally well for fisher.

The fisher (courtesy Mark Brown)

WOLVES

Wolf trapping, at least in the United States, seems to be only a remembered activity. At one time, wolves were found over most of what is now the United States, but the few remaining animals are now limited to parks and some parts of Minnesota, although occasional sightings are reported in the more remote parts of other northern plains states.

The decline of wolf population in the United States is primarily due to the wolf's inability to coexist with man. Wolves are about as prolific as any other canine; they have an annual litter of 6 to 10 young born in March or early April. These canine furbearers weigh from 75 to 125 pounds and their primary prey are large animals such as elk, deer, or moose. Unfortunately, it may attack domestic stock, and has thus been persecuted by man. Some wolves still thrive in the back country of the Canadian wilderness and Alaska and thereby provide some trapping opportunity. Trapping techniques that work on coyote will work on wolves as well.

WOLVERINE

Similar to the coyote and mink, the wolverine has an entire folk history surrounding it. According to Indian legends and other stories, the wolverine is capable of magic insofar as avoiding traps. In actuality, the wolverine is probably a moderately intelligent animal which, like its weasel cousins, is capable of prodigious consumption of foodstuffs and is known to foul an area with its odor. Beyond that, the wolverine is by no stretch of the imagination a supernatural being.

The wolverine is found almost exclusively in the extreme northern part of the United States and in Canada. The wolverine will have an average length of 30 to 36 inches and weigh from 25 to 30 pounds, although extraordinary specimens much larger than this have been reported and have occasionally been mistaken for small bears. The pelt of the wolverine is very shaggy, dark brown in color with two or more stripes running from the shoulder down to the back. The wolverine does not bear much of a resemblance to its weasel cousins, although it is, like other weasels, ferocious and possessed of a voracious appetite.

Catches of wolverine are undoubtedly unusual, as the animals are not numerous. The average litter of a wolverine is two to five. Somewhat like the fisher or marten, even where populations are relatively good, there are not very many wolverines. The occasional trapped wolverine will bring a very good price, especially in today's improved market for wild pelts. The fur is highly sought for trim and glove lining as it is one of the very few long-haired furs that does not freeze and break readily.

The few people who actually set traps specifically for the wolverine ordinarily use some sort of carrion bait in multiple sets of large leghold traps. The wolverine, very much like the badger, is an inordinately tough customer when trapped and should be approached only with the greatest of caution. Wolverines are usually treated like badgers when skinned — that is, they are open pelted and stretched flat as nearly square as possible. However, may fur buyers prefer the cased pelt as far as wolverines are concerned.

GROUNDHOG

The groundhog, or hedgehog or woodchuck, is not a furbearer in the ordinary sense. However, the animal deserves a certain amount of attention simply because it is so widespread and many, many trappers are able to gain access to private land to trap furbearers because of the desire of landowners to rid the area of groundhogs. The groundhog is a pest to virtually all landowners. The holes they dig are large and

The common groundhog or woodchuck.

numerous. They consume vegetation intended for other animals or as crops. Of course, the dens are a hazard to livestock.

There is no real trick involved in catching the groundhog using the steel leghold trap. A No. 1½ or 2 long spring or double spring will work. These animals do not appear to be the slightest bit trap shy and will take almost any bait. Where the trap is legal, a No. 120 conibear set as a killer trap will work beautifully on groundhogs.

Groundhog flesh is very good to eat, bearing a strong resemblance to raccoon. The animal should be trimmed of fat before cooking.

5 Basic Sets

SOME PRACTICAL CONSIDERATIONS

Making effective sets is a skill which is developed and gradually refined through experience, but the time lost through trial and error can be reduced by an understanding of some of the basics of set making. The tips which follow apply as general rules to all of the sets and variations of sets which are described in this book. Observing these pointers while making sets will result in better catches.

Cover the trap so that there is no interference with the working of the pan or the grip once the jaws have closed. To avoid trouble, be certain there is nothing under the pan to prevent it from dropping and releasing the trigger properly. The accompanying illustration shows how a pan cover works to keep crud from getting under the pan. Too much covering or clumps of covering may keep the trap from closing quickly or may keep the jaws from holding fast. Cover lightly with shredded materials which will fall away when the trap closes. Covering with dirt or leaves may present problems if the cover freezes into a solid piece that will keep the trap from functioning properly. Some trappers avoid freezing by using glycerine as antifreeze but the glycerine may alert a trap-shy furbearer. Others cover traps with chaff or dirt from anthills, neither of which freezes readily. Still others crumble horse or cow manure rather than dirt over the trap.

Trappers should try to anticipate the direction of the furbearer's approach and set the trap so the animal does not step over a jaw but rather steps over the hinge onto the pan. If the animal steps on a jaw, there is a good chance the leg will be popped from the trap.

The trap should always be set with the thought in mind that there is only one small spot where the furbearer can step and make the trap work. To increase the chances of the furbearer hitting that precise spot, trappers should use guide stakes or step overs such as sticks and stones to help head the animal to one path right over the pan.

Drags are devices to slow down a trapped animal. Solidly staking a land-set trap is not recommended because almost any animal that can get resistance will pull free and escape. The drag should provide enough resistance to exhaust the animal and keep it from getting too far, yet not permit a solid pull. Some trappers wire traps to willowy saplings to restrict the animal's movement without creating too much solid resistance.

The sense of smell is very highly developed in most animals and all furbearers. Every effort should be made to avoid human scent tainting the set. Trappers should not use scented aftershave or perfumed essences. Traps and trapping clothing should be kept away from house odors or contamination by fuel or smoke, as from a garage. Trappers should have no more contact with the set than absolutely necessary. To reduce body contact in the area, many trappers squat rather than kneel. If they must kneel, they use a kneeling sheet.

Finally, trappers can reduce problems with their sets by engaging in a bit of secrecy. Many trappers tell no one where their trapline is located and check it as casually as possible from as great a distance as they can.

THE SETS

All of the sets a trapper uses are actually variations on a few basic themes. These variations are only limited by the trapper's imagination. In fact, varieties are mentioned in Chapter 4.

Basic Blind Set

The basic blind set is at once the simplest and yet most difficult set to make. This set, if the name is to be believed, is tossed out blindly without bait or seeming regard for furbearer activity. In fact, the blind set is made in a place where, because of sign such as tracks, the trapper believes there is an extremely high chance of the animal appearing and stepping into the trap.

The blind set is most often set where there is an established trail or track of furbearers. Once these are located, it is a matter of placing the traps with care and taking steps to "assist" the animal into the trap or guide a foot onto the pan. This is usually done with the assistance of some variation of the guide stake. If a constriction can be found to assure that the animal will pass over a certain spot, and stay on the trail, the trapper has found a good site. To narrow the precise spot on the trail where the trap is hidden, the trapper will use a version of the guide stake called the trail breaker or step over log. Actually, the best set, although somewhat costly in terms of traps, is a set using two step overs with traps on the trail between and on either side of the step overs. The furbearer will approach the obstructions, too small to bother going around, and so they step over; the properly placed traps should get the furbearer coming, going, or in between.

An added plus to the step over stakes is the fact that they can be used as the drags on the traps. Probably better drag equipment, however, are the grapnels either manufactured for this purpose or fashioned from size 000 treble hooks used for snag fishing. These fishing

Obstruction set (wet and dry)

111

Trail set

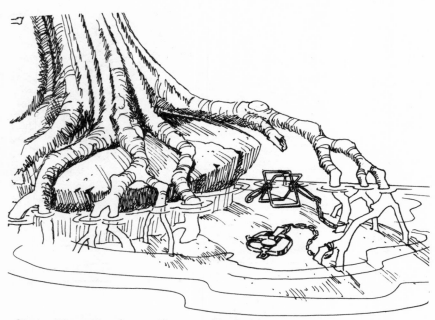

Obstruction set using conibear and leghold.

112

Bridge set

Spring set

113

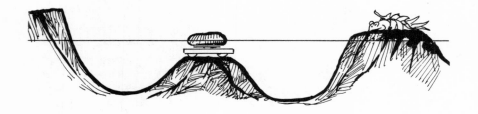

Cross section of spring set

Scent post set

hooks are easily adapted by making the barbs flat with pliers and removing one hook so those remaining can lie flat.

Variations of the blind set include those limited only by the collective imagination of the trappers. The accompanying illustrations show six variations: the obstruction set, the trail set, the bridge or culvert set, the spring set, the log-crossing set, and the diving set. A common characteristic of these sets is that they are placed where sign or observation indicates furbearers should appear and that obstructions (e.g., step-over logs, rocks, or walls) are used to narrow the places where the furbearer can place its foot. Scent may be used to increase activity or to cause the furbearers to linger in the area of a blind set.

A final blind set meriting special mention is the scent-post set. The well-known trait of canines marking territory with urine and returning regularly is exploited by this set. Many trappers set more than one trap 15 inches from the post and thereby make multiple catches.

Interval Set

The interval set is very effective for skunks and canine furbearers. It can be made by using a series of carefully placed stones surrounding a bait with scent. The bait (cracklings, bacon rinds, rotten eggs) is placed

Interval set

115

in the center of large stones that are no more than 12 inches apart. The gap between each pair of stones harbors a No. 1½ trap with either a drag or grapnel; a *long* chain or wire is used to get trapped animals clear of the area. The stones, of course, serve to guide the furbearer over the pan of the trap as it seeks out the bait. This set can be modified as the trapper's ingenuity is inclined. Some trappers might choose to make this a multi-entrance cubby set by covering it with weathered cardboard or other available material. One unique feature of the interval set is that the occasional animal that actually makes it to the bait without being trapped must again cross the trap to exit. This set often amounts to a "repeater" with several animals being taken in one night. The interval trap will take raccoon, possum, weasel, and canine furbearers.

Baited Sets

The sets that use bait will include the carcass set, the floating set, and the persimmon or gob set, depending on the bait, and all of the cubby sets where bait is used. Bait of various kinds has been discussed elsewhere.

Cubby set

Cubby Sets

The term cubby set is broadly used to describe any number of sets that take advantage of the furbearer's curiosity and tendency to explore openings in rocks, logs, or the exposed roots of trees. Cubby sets may be called exposed root sets or hollow log sets, but all are basically the same: an enclosure that will arouse a furbearer's curiosity, obstructions such as step overs or guide stakes, and appropriately placed traps. Cubby sets are used with or without lure or bait.

Hole Sets

Sets using a hole are actually variations of cubbies. As the accompanying illustrations show, the hole sets are designed to bring the animal close and then to confine its approach by means of guides and step overs.

Dirt hole set

Drowning Sets

Most sets for aquatic or semiaquatic furbearers can and should be drowning sets. In addition to those sets already mentioned for such furbearers, the diving set, the run set, the platform set, and the slide or entry set are adaptable to a drowning arrangement. Note that all drowning sets have in common a cable or line attached to the trap to lead the furbearer into water once trapped, a device to keep the furbearer from reversing once in too deep, and a tangle stake for the trap chain to keep the animal under water.

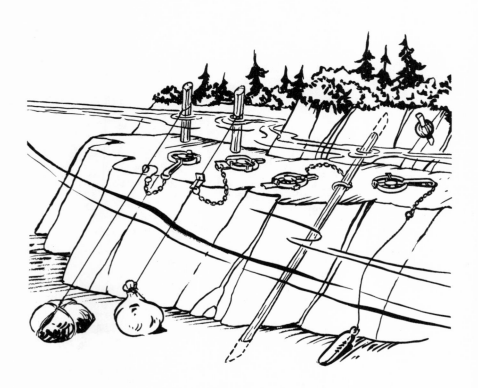

Drowning sets

UNUSUAL SETS

No anthology of trapping nor any trapping bull session would be complete without a reference to a few odd sets or unusual catches. *Traplines North,* a fictionalized version of a trapper's journal, relates a story about catching a great horned owl in a trap set for lynx. These last four sets are unusual but are used occasionally by trappers all over North America. All are designed to deal with the unusual circumstance or the especially trap-wary furbearer.

Wing Set

The wing set is an adaptation of a bait set that appeals to the visual sense rather than smell. The wing of any bird will do — a quail, grouse, duck, even a sparrow, although the latter may be too small to attract much attention. The wing should be tied with monofilament fishing line at the ball joint that formerly attached to the shoulder of the bird. Leaving two or three feet of line to allow a free swing, the wing is attached to an open branch to hang within six or seven feet off the ground. The wing should be hung in a place likely to catch at least an occasional breeze to make it flutter and therefore be more prone to catch a furbearer's eye and arouse its curiosity.

The trap itself — or traps — should be set immediately under the wing and covered lightly. The object of this set is to arouse the curiosity of a passing furbearer who will come to investigate and pace or walk on hind legs under the wing until it steps onto the pan. The wing set will work on all of the cats — bobcats and lynx — plus coyote, fox, and raccoon.

Shiny Object

The shiny object set is designed almost solely for raccoons, although it will take an occasional muskrat or mink. The set, made in an area known to be well populated with raccoons, consists of a shiny object — a cheap pocket mirror, aluminum foil, or even an old stainless steel teaspoon — and a leghold trap. The shiny object is attached directly to the pan of the trap and serves, in a way, as bait. This "bait" also serves as a sight attraction rather than appealing to the sense of smell, and curiosity leads the furbearer to investigate. Clear, shallow water is, of course, a necessity and a couple of guide rocks to limit the number of approaches will greatly increase the productivity of this set. A bright phase of the moon will aid the productivity also, providing light to make the object shine.

Wing set

Campfire Set

Coyote, fox, raccoon, skunk, and possum regularly visit old, cold campfire sites looking for scraps that may have been left or tossed into the fire. Such a campsite may become as regular a part of these furbearers' rounds as a small dump, especially where the area is used heavily by campers. The campfire set takes advantage of this natural affinity by setting a whole series of traps all around the old fire. Of all the unusual sets, this one actually uses bait calculated to appeal to smell or taste. The campfire set is usually baited with any meaty scent bait —

bacon grease, ham fat, entrails, or any of the musk lures. All of the gaps between the larger stones placed at intervals around the cold campfire are potential trap sites. Six or more traps might ring the fire and several may take furbearers in a given setting. A drag or grapnel is best on this multiple set because the trapper will want the quarry to clear the area once caught and so avoid alerting other furbearers who may approach.

Fake Trap

When the occasional animal has become clever enough to recognize a trap-bearing cubby, some trappers use a second trap, in effect, as a guide device to put the furbearer on the primary, hidden trap. The cubby is prepared, baited if desired, and a second, hidden trap put into place. Rather than a guide stake or rock, the second trap is set and placed in more or less clear view for the furbearer to see. The trap-wary furbearer will avoid the visible trap and sometimes will go so far as to scatter dirt or leaves on it before walking on the pan of the real trap. This is a good set for fox, coyote, and raccoon.

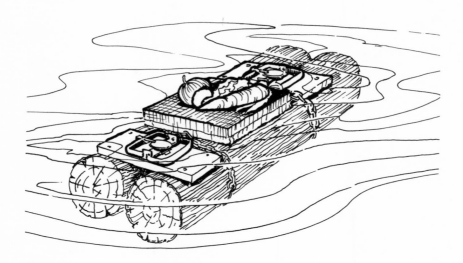

Float set for muskrats

Rat Trap Killer Set

With pressures mounting for some humane traps — those that kill quickly or instantly either from a lethal blow or drowning — the use of the simple rat trap as a killer trap has gained popularity. This killer set is designed solely for muskrats although an occasional mink or nutria will wander into it. One peculiarity of the set is that it is essentially a water set and yet the entire trap itself is clear of the water to prevent the water from cushioning the bar's blow.

Attached to a stake to prevent the trapped furbearer from escaping, the set is made by driving the stake into the creek or pond bottom to a position with the trap frame just touching the water. Baited with carrots or parsnips, the trap will attract muskrats which, if they touch the pan, will be fatally injured by the bar and held at the trap site.

Many trappers who are aware of the vitality and determined resistance of muskrats are skeptical of a rat trap's ability to kill so large an animal, but the set works extremely well and also is relatively inexpensive. Anyone who has accidentally touched off one of these traps has enough memories (and maybe a broken finger or two) to persuade him that the set is powerful.

Prolonged exposure to the elements may cause the staples in the rat trap to pull out. Replacing them with brass screws or wire run through and back over will solve the problem.

Spring run set for mink.

6 Handling the Catch from Trap to Market

CARE OF PELTS — FROM SKINNING TO CURED PELT

Without question, the handling of pelts is the most important step in a trapper's regimen. Just as a trap that does not hold fast can render the best set unproductive, fumbling the job of caring for any pelt, even the most valuable, can render it worthless. Great care should be taken in every step in the handling of pelts.

Sale of pelts is covered in the following section, but one comment is timely here. When the trapper learns to whom he will be selling his furs, some effort should be made to learn how the buyer prefers his pelts presented. Some animals are generally case pelted; others, usually open pelted. But the generalizations do not mean a thing if the buyer in question prefers another way. Remember that some buyers have stayed with the older, open pelting on raccoon, muskrat, skunk, and bobcats, and this preference should be honored. In the same vein, many buyers prefer to purchase certain animals in the round, or unskinned; this is especially true with beaver, which are extremely difficult to skin and even more difficult to skin properly. If the buyer wants to skin beaver himself, the trapper should know about it and act on this knowledge. Finally, a certain number of buyers will accept and actually seem to prefer pelts frozen and not stretched and cured; this can be a time saver for the trapper and should be information the trapper considers.

Handling of pelts begins in the field; in fact, it begins with the animal still in the trap. Obviously, holes from bullets or other sources reduce the value of a pelt. Care should be exercised to prevent any such damage to the pelt. Likewise, large bruised places will reduce the pelt's value. Animals taken alive in traps should be killed with as little damage as possible. A sharp blow or bullet to the head are the best ways.

Animals that are frozen — either in solid ice or with ice crystals in the pelt — should *never* be pulled from the ice or have the ice yanked from their fur. If necessary, the animal should be chopped from the ice and taken to a warm spot to thaw. All ice crystals should be thawed; any temptation to crumble, pull, or comb the ice out should be resisted because this sort of removal invariably loosens some hair; a buyer will spot it and quite understandably reduce the price.

Blood should be kept free from the fur. If blood does contact the fur, it should be wiped or rinsed off while it is still wet if possible. If it is not possible, care is necessary to get the blood out as combing or pulling may tear hair loose. Gently crumble or wash out any mud.

The animal should be at room temperature when skinning begins and should be thawed to avoid tears and improper incisions; a frozen carcass is difficult to pelt. As a matter of fact, animals still warm from body temperature will not have the skin "set" on the carcass and the pelt will slip off very easily after the knife is used only to make incisions, not for working the skin from the body.

There are two ways in which an animal is skinned, either open or cased. These types of skinning will result in three types of cured pelts: the standard cased pelt (raccoon and skunk), the square stretched pelt (badger and wolverine) and the round stretched pelt (beaver). We first deal with the cased and then with the two open-skinned animals.

Case skinning an animal is much easier if the animal is at a convenient level and preferably hanging upside down. This can be accomplished in several ways. Skinning gambrels especially designed for holding furbearers are available and work very well. However, anything that will hold the hind foot up will work. Some trappers get by very well using a No. 1 trap to hold the animal by one foot and permitting the carcass to swing and move as the trapper desires. The accompanying photos of the skinning process show a raccoon held aloft by a piece of double-looped baling twine. Others rig their own gambrels of large nails on a sturdy beam or tree trunk. One trapper at least uses a clothespin-type fishing stringer to hold the animal. With any of the homemade approaches, the nail or fish stringer goes between the bone and the large tendon of the upper rear leg and holds at the knee.

A word here about knives. Whether the trapper chooses to invest a lot of money in custom-made knives or to limp along with a discount house pocketknife, he should make every effort to keep a very keen edge on the steel. Far fewer cut fingers result from a sharp knife slipping along than from a dull knife being sawed and forced. Also, a keen edge will not be overused and result in cut pelts as will a duller blade.

The skinning process begins with a cut from heel to heel below the vent. Note the double-looped cord supporting the raccoon.

The skin is cut loose from the leg and worked away.

The relatively few outdoor types who know how to put an edge on a knife is remarkable. "Put an edge on" is the correct phrase because even a moderately successful trapper will not be able to keep the knife keen; he must continually restore the edge.

The trapper should acquire a good sharpening stone — a washita, preferably — and learn how to use it. A dash of oil on the stone and a few strokes on both the coarse and fine sides of the stone and the knife will be ready. Semihollow ground knives should be set at a 20-degree angle from the stone and pushed, base to tip, away in a motion that looks as though the knife will be cutting a thin slice from the stone. Flat ground knives such as pocketknives should be angled to fit the incline of the point, but the motion is exactly the same.

For the benefit of those persons who have some difficulty getting the edge of the knife at the proper angle, there is now available a device called the honemaster that is widely marketed and that will set the proper angle without any margin for error.

Once the animal is held in position, trappers should take a very sharp knife and cut a slit from one heel of the furbearer to the other

The bone is stripped from the tail very carefully.

heel, passing the cut between the tail and the anus. The next step is to cut the hide from the initial incision around the anus and genitals to leave a small patch that will remain on the carcass; this patch will also contain the musk glands and in the case of beaver, the castors that should be treated carefully as they will later be removed and used for lure. If the furbearer is a skunk, the anus might be tied off at this time.

The skin is then worked around the legs and cut free of the legs at the knees. If the tail is to be kept, the tail part of the pelt will be either stripped from the bone or split depending on the species and the buyer's preferences. Splitting is done by slipping the knife, sharp edge up, from the base of the tail to the tip or until the bone pops loose; this is always done on the underside of the tail. Stripping is accomplished by working the bone loose in one hand and gently pulling until the bone comes out. A tail stripper that is a pair of matched sticks with a center hole as illustrated can help in this process; a small adjustable wrench also will work.

Once the legs and tail are free, the skin is pulled off something like reversing and pulling off a sock. Where the animal is still warm, the pelt will not have set, and pulling the skin off will be very easy. In any event, the knife is used only to help the pelt along, not to cut the hide off. At the front legs, and especially the head, the knife will be used to loosen the hide. Great care should be taken to get all of the pelt, including the ears and the areas around the eyes, lips, and nose.

Claws left on pelts are pretty much a thing of the past, but a few buyers still insist upon certain animals being pelted with the claws remaining. Trappers who sell to buyers who prefer claws left on may find the following helpful. Claws may be left on the wild felines, mink, foxes, coyote, fishers, and marten. To leave these on, skin the animal as usual, except of course do not cut the skin loose at the lower hind leg. Using a pair of skinning pliers, clamp the bone off as close as possible to the foot-pad of one hind leg. Continue with the skinning operation as usual but rather than cutting the skin loose at the foreleg, clamp the bone off at the pads, also. The last part of the animal to be skinned this way is the left hind leg.

Once the pelt has been removed from the carcass, the carcass can be set aside and a preliminary fleshing of the pelt performed. Slip the pelt over a stretching board — not a wire frame — or a fleshing beam and use a dull knife or edge of a teaspoon to remove any flesh or fat that might have clung to the pelt in skinning. Any excess oil or other residue can be removed at this time also.

The case-skinned animal has the pelt reversed from it — something like a sock being pulled off.

The pelt is pulled down to the front legs which have already
had the paws removed.

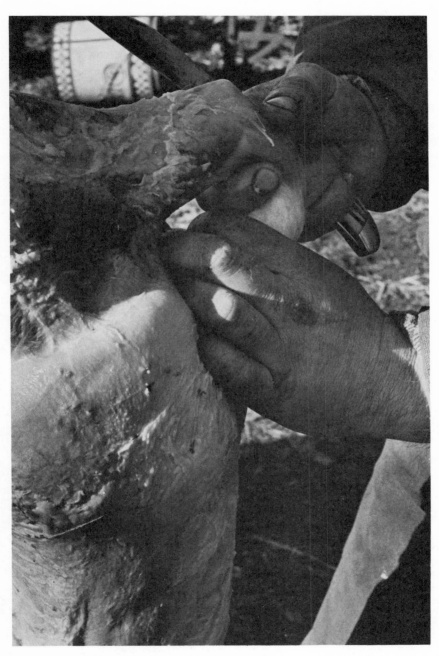

The front leg is pulled through the hide.

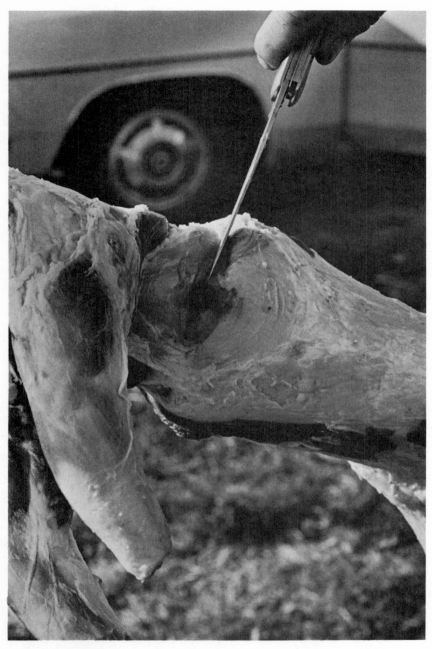

The hide is pulled down and over the head and the ears are removed.

The skinner works the hide over the head below the ears.

Every bit of the facial fur is carefully worked off the animal.

The pelt is now completely clear of the carcass and ready to
be reversed.

The pelt is reversed to its original position.

The end result: one very large, prime raccoon pelt. (photo series courtesy of Russ Reagan of the Missouri Department of Conservation)

Once the initial fleshing is done, a pelt can be pulled onto a proper-sized stretching board or drying frame for curing. The accompanying chart will give the appropriate-sized frames. The temptation to stretch the pelt as tightly as a drumhead should be resisted. Overstretching will damage the pelts, making the fur seem thin, and no fur buyer will be fooled by the extra size. Stretch the pelt tight and clamp or tack it in place; then permit it to dry at a moderate temperature (approximately 60 to 70 degrees Fahrenheit). Pelts may take a week or more to dry properly; with fatty animals such as raccoon, possum, and skunk, wiping the hide may be necessary to remove oil and hasten drying. Pelts should never be removed from the frames or boards prior to being completely dry as they will develop a wizened look which reduces the value.

Two final comments are necessary before going to open-skinned animals, one on choice of stretchers and another on the stretching itself.

Stretching boards have been around for centuries and probably will continue to be around as long as their use is acceptable to fur buyers. However, as use of the wire frame increases, more buyers are showing a preference for pelts dried on them because of the greater uniformity. In addition, the frames are light, more compact and easier to hang. It now appears that use of the wire frame, inexpensive as it is, is becoming more than a mere matter of taste.

Some cased pelts are dried fur side out. The choice is supposed to be based on whether the quality of the pelt can be determined by inspecting the tail and the fur visible at the bottom. Since virtually all furbearer pelts can suffer some greater or lesser damage from rubbing and fighting, this does not seem entirely accurate, but the fact remains that some pelts are dried with the hide inside. Those dried fur side out include the canine group (coyote, fox, and wolf) and the feline (bobcat and lynx) plus the marten, fisher, and wolverine. These animals are initially stretched as any other pelt, hide side out, and are permitted to dry for a day or so, then reversed while still flexible. If the drying has gone too far to reverse the pelt, the pelt may be softened a little with water to make the switch possible.

Open pelts are desirable on beaver, badger, and sometimes otter. Skinning a beaver is a remarkably difficult task for the beginner as the pelt seems to be part of the carcass rather than a covering. Beaver pelts are cut, inch by inch, from the carcass; this can be very time consuming. Many fur buyers prefer to buy the whole beaver or buy "in the round," because very few people can skin a beaver properly. Most trappers who have ever skinned a beaver would be receptive to a sale in the round just to avoid the time-consuming and exasperating task. Skinning a beaver begins with a cut from the chin to the tail and removing the feet and the tail. The pelt is pulled up and cut away from the carcass until the legs are pushed through, pulled and cut much as a case pelt is reversed. Fleshing the beaver pelt can be a chore also, as the gristle and flesh are stubbornly attached to the beaver pelt. The only way to remove clinging fat and gristle is to use a fleshing beam and elbow grease with a dull blade such as an ax head. The beaver pelt is stretched round or oval; the classic method is to use a wooden ring and leather thongs to attach the pelt, but the more practical technique is to nail the pelt to a sheet of plywood, hide side out. Be certain the fur is completely dry, since prolonged contact between the wood and wet fur can cause the fur to deteriorate. Nail the pelt in place snugly but not tightly, allowing the pelt to shrink as it dries. The nails should be about one and one half to two inches apart. The leg skin should be pulled into the pelt after the pelt is stretched, in order to close the small holes.

Badger is skinned the same as beaver, but is dried square. This is done by tacking the pelt to plywood the same as with beaver but stretched square.

SELLING THE CATCH

Selling pelts always presents a problem. The fur market is very nearly a pure free enterprise-type arrangement with events and moods hundreds of miles away — sometimes on other continents having a great influence on the local market. Consequently, the marketplace produces an intimidating effect on the seller. Then there are the wide fluctuations that result from contracts being met, drawing near, or not being met. Trying to time proper entry into and exit from the market can be unnerving.

The most common approach to marketing pelts is contacting a local dealer, presenting the pelts, and attempting to strike a bargain. The problem, of course, is trying to determine a fair price. The buyer is just one link in the chain beginning with the trapper and reaching all the way to the retailer. Avoiding the middleman by going directly to the wholesalers or tanners would be nice for the trapper, but this is difficult to do. Many trappers attempt to go around the local buyer by dealing by freight or mail with the larger buyers on the East Coast. These companies offer very attractive prices partially because they have cut the middleman out but also because they tend to grade very rigorously. The local buyer is ordinarily the best bet, especially for the small-time or hobby trapper. The local buyer is there, usually year-round, and can offer cash in a hurry. He also may be a valuable source of information about market conditions. Local buyers are either respected men of integrity, or they are not buyers very long.

The author and local buyer Vernon Rackers inspect a prime raccoon pelt.

Another approach to selling furs that is becoming increasingly popular is the fur auction. Such auctions usually are sponsored by local trappers' clubs and occasionally by state conservation commissions or local conservation organizations. These auctions are designed to present many trappers' catches at one time for the mutual benefit of buyers and trappers. Trappers get the advantage of a fair market price for their cache of pelts being established by open competition. From the buyer's standpoint, he might well make purchases for an entire year's contract in one day. The cost of the auction is usually paid by a per pelt charge levied on each trapper participating. The fee is usually modest with a common rate being five or ten cents per pelt except squirrel tails. Good sources of information on the details concerning such auctions are local conservation offices and outdoors writers for local newspapers.

Of course, in selling the pelts the trapper must make every effort to make his catch as attractive as possible. This means combing and brushing the furs and having everything in order, perhaps graded to size. If the trapper uses the frozen pelt method rather than stretching and curing, the furs should be partially thawed so examination of the pelts can be facilitated.

The meat of several furbearers is edible, ranging in quality from good to delicacy. Possum, raccoon, muskrats, and beaver are all desirable table fare. A trapper who is even moderately successful will have far more meat than he can use himself. After a quick check of the applicable codes to be certain that the sale of skinned furbearer carcasses is legal in a jurisdiction, the trapper lets the word out the he has game to sell; usually a market will develop quickly.

Prices are pretty much catch-as-catch-can, but $2 to $3 for a possum, $1 to $1.50 for a muskrat, and $2.50 to $3 for a raccoon or beaver is a good place to start pricing.

CARE OF PELTS EPILOGUE — HOME TANNING

Pelts sold to fur buyers are always raw, whether frozen or stretched and cured. On occasion, the trapper may have the desire to tan a few pelts. This can be done easily with splendid results.

All of the necessary materials can be readily acquired. The necessities include hydrated lime, neatsfoot oil, and naphtha thinner (a.k.a. Benzine), available where paint is sold; boric acid and alum, available in drugstores; iodine-free salt from any grocery; and sawdust found wherever saws are dusted. Plastic pails are ideal for holding the tanning solution. This solution is not good for the hands, so wearing rubber gloves is recommended.

The first step is to remove any flesh or fat that might still cling to the hide. This is nothing more than the scraping step of stretching and curing. When tanning, there is no question about the use of salt to hasten fat and flesh removal; do it. Salt the moist pelt moderately to heavily, roll it up hide side in, and stash it for a day or so. The salt will make final fat and flesh removal very simple.

The second step is degreasing. Find a location outside and away from flames to degrease the scraped pelts. Rub the naphtha into both the hair and hide sides. Then rub sawdust into both sides to remove the naphtha and dissolved grease. Shake the sawdust out carefully and rinse the pelt thoroughly in water.

(Furbearer pelts are very rarely stripped of hair, but if this is desired, the removal is timely after step two; otherwise go on to the third step. Hair removal is accomplished by soaking the pelt in a solution of four ounces hydrated lime and eight ounces wood ashes to a gallon of water until the hair begins to slip or pull free. The hair is then scraped off and the hairless skin rinsed thoroughly and soaked in a boric acid solution overnight to neutralize any residual lime.)

The third step, whether hair is on or off, involves soaking the skin in a tanning solution for one week. The tanning solution is eight ounces

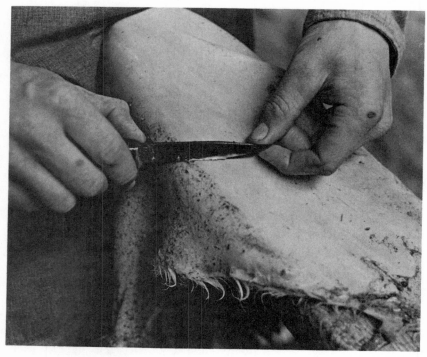

Final scraping to remove fat and flesh.

Degreasing with naphtha and drying with sawdust.

iodine-free salt and four ounces alum per gallon of water. The skin should be completely covered by the solution, which must be stirred frequently. At the end of a week, remove the pelt, rinse, and hang until merely damp. Rub neat's-foot oil into the hide side and let it begin to dry. During the drying process, stretch or pull the pelt in all directions over a fleshing beam or sawhorse to promote suppleness.

The skin of the pelt will have varying thicknesses from very thick at the neck to very thin on the belly. If consistent thickness is necessary or desirable, the differences can be removed with coarse sandpaper.

Soaking in tanning solution.

The hide is softened by rubbing in neat's-foot oil.

Suppleness is promoted by stretching in all directions.

The finished product. (photo series courtesy of the Missouri
Department of Conservation)

7 A Few Final Words—Ethics

Having considered the various mechanical aspects of trapping, the trapper's attitude deserves discussion. In a time when hunting, and even fishing, is increasingly under pressure from "friends of wildlife," trapping is bound to be a target for criticism. Every trapper owes it to himself, to other trappers, and to trapping as a sport or vocation to reduce this criticism by conducting himself in as commendable a fashion as possible. Certain patterns of behavior evolve and become essentially a code of trapping ethics which, similar to other sets of manners and etiquette, is merely common sense and consideration for others.

First a trapper should never trap an area without permission. Obviously, if the land is public with access to trappers, permission is tacitly given. Private land is another matter. Permission should always be secured, well in advance, and never taken for granted. It should be noted that entry onto private land without permission is now a misdemeanor in many jurisdictions.

Second, traps should be checked regularly, often, and preferably early in the day. Many jurisdictions have laws requiring checking, and even where it is not law, it is strongly recommended. One struggling, apparently suffering animal spotted by a nontrapper can cause problems. Also, trapping carries with it a respect for the quarry and that respect includes a reluctance to have the animal endure any more confinement than necessary.

Third, the trapper should obey all game laws, both in letter and spirit. This, of course, involves releasing animals that are protected or are nontarget species but also includes not making sets where these animals might easily be caught. Be certain that all traps are pulled by the end of the season and use only clearly lawful equipment.

Fourth, select bait and lure carefully to catch target animals only. Do not use meat where dogs and other pets might find it.

Fifth, use proper traps for the animals sought. Killer-type traps are best where they can be used. Avoid traps that are too small for the game and permit escape; wring offs are a loss to all concerned.

Sixth, report game violations. There is nothing cute, clever, or ad mirable about a thief or a cheat. A game violator is one or both of these. Trappers cannot afford to shelter any violators.

Seventh, release unwanted animals promptly. Return any captured pets with condolences and offers of help with any expenses.

Eighth, conduct your trapping to avoid offending others. Keep traps out of sight and do not litter the area with trash or animal carcasses.

Ninth, do not disturb other traps. Obviously, releasing an animal or carrying off a trap is stealing. But checking the line can adversely affect the catch, also. And remember, you do no one a favor by displaying a trapped animal.

Finally, learn all there is to know about the quarry and sport. The more proficient a trapper is, the less likely he is to suffer with wring-offs, exposure to the nontrapping public, or any other unintentional breach of manners.

Appendix

TRAPPING SUPPLIERS AND ORGANIZATIONS

There is no way to locate all suppliers and trappers' organizations because they are widely scattered and include lots of more or less casual groups and suppliers. However, the following basic list should be of value.

TRAPS, SUPPLIES, ETC.

The lists below break trappers' supplies into three categories. Of course, the dealers may change lines from time to time, but whatever the trapper needs should be found here somewhere.

FULL LINES OF SUPPLIES

Mike Ayers
Cortez Route
Dove Creek, Colorado 61324

L.L. Bean
Freeport, Maine 04033

Blake and Lamb
Box 218
Cambridge, New York 12816

Blue Valley Fur Buyers
and Supply
500 South 4th
Beatrice, Nebraska 68310

Burnham Brothers
Box 100c
Marble Falls, Texas 68654

O.L. Butcher Trapping Supplies
Shushan, New York 12873

Campbell Cage Company
Box 545
Campbell, California 95008

Oden Corr
405 West 3rd Street
Miller, South Dakota 57362

Cronk's Outdoor Supplies
Wiscasset, Maine 04578

E.J. Dailey
Box 38c
Union Hill, New York 14563

Hancock Trap Company
110 South 19th Street
Hot Springs, South Dakota 57747

Havahart (Allcock Mfg. Company)
Box 551
Ossining, New York 10562

Stanley Hawbaker and Sons
258 Hawbaker Drive South
Fort Loudon, Pennsylvania 17224

Mardian's
Box 370
Mobridge, South Dakota 57601

M&M Furs
Bridgewater, South Dakota 57319

Mesler Supply
Box 357 L
West Burlington, Iowa 52655

MHF
Box 8918
Moscow, Idaho 83843

Mid-States Sporting Goods
Luverne, Minnesota 56156

Mustang Manufacturing Company
Box 10880
Houston, Texas 77018

National Live Trap Corporation
Box 302
Tomahawk, Wisconsin 54487

Northwest Trappers' Supplies
Box 408
Owatonna, Minnesota 55060

Northwoods Trapline Supplies
Thief River Falls, Minnesota 56701

Oberto Trap Company
Box 88
Iron Belt, Wisconsin 54536

P&S Trapping Supplies
Star Route 4, Box 109
Miller, South Dakota 57362

Pete Rickard
Cobleskill, New York 12043

Don Sieverding
Spencer, South Dakota 57374

Southeastern Outdoor Supply
Route 3 Box 503
Basset, Virginia 24055

Sullivan's Sure Catch Traps
Box 1241
Valdosta, Georgia 31601

Taylor Fur Company
227 East Market
Louisville, Kentucky 40202

Raymond Thompson Company
15815 2nd Place
Lynwood, Washington 98036

Tomahawk Live Trap Company
Box 323
Tomahawk, Wisconsin 54487

Verleen Trapper Supply
RR1
Nashville, Kansas 67112

Woodstream Corporation
Box 327
Lititz, Pennsylvania 17543

SPECIALISTS IN PREDATOR CALLS

Ed Bauer Fur Company
RFD No. 1
Smithsboro, Illinois 62284

Circe Calls
Box 697
Goodyear, Arizona 85338

P.S. Olt Company
Box 550
Pekin, Illinois 61554

The Song Dogs
3836 South Taft Hill Road
Fort Collins, Colorado 80521

Thompson Wildlife Calls
Box 8002
Boise, Idaho 38707

Weems Wild Calls
500 South 7th Street
Fort Smith, Arkansas 72901

SPECIALISTS IN LURES

Carman's Animal Lures
Box TT
New Milford, Pennsylvania 18834

E.J. Dailey Lures
Box 38
Union Hill, New York 14563

Garold Weiland
Glenham, South Dakota 57631

ORGANIZATIONS

National Trappers' Association
Box 3667
Bloomington, Illinois 61701

Alberta Trappers'
Central Association
Box 259
Worsley, Alberta T0H3W0

Bay State Trappers' Association
155 Williams Road
Concord, Massachusetts 01742

California Trappers' Association
Box 3004
Redding, California 96001

Colorado Trappers' Association
3836 South Taft Hill Road
Fort Collins, Colorado 80926

East Central Illinois Fur Takers
Route 1 Box 41
Onarga, Illinois 60955

Indiana State Trappers' Association
RR 2
Campbellsburg, Indiana 47108

Pennsylvania Trappers' Association
R.D. #3 Box 157
Gettysburg, Pennsylvania 17325

South Central Trappers' Association
P.O. Box 4-2474
Anchorage, Alaska 99059

Southeast Ohio Fur Takers
Route 3
McConnersville, Ohio 43756

Upper Catskill Fur Takers
Allem Road
Jefferson, New York 12093

Virginia Trappers' Association
P.O. Box 14131
Norfolk, Virginia 23518

Wisconsin Trappers' Association
1912 South 13th Street
Sheboygan, Wisconsin 53081

Index

Acrylics, 33
Air pistols, 49
Air rifles, 48-49
American Sable, 81
Anthropomorphism, 4
Axes, 38

Badger, 52, 86-87, 107, 138
Bags, 37-38
Bait, 49-51
Baited sets, 116
Baiting, 19
  Prohibition, 19
Bambi syndrome, 4
Basket, 39
Benzine, 141
Beaver, 1, 2, 6, 15, 20, 23, 52, 93-97, 138
  Colony, 96
  Lodge, 96
Blind set, 110-111
Bobcat, 20, 29, 52, 87-90
Brambles, 6
Bridge set, 79, 113
Buyers, 139

Campfire set, 120-121
Canadian-type stretcher, 58
Carrying capacity, 1, 2
Case skinning, 124-137
Castors, 52-53, 97
Channels, 15
Claws, 128
Clothing, 54-56
Coil spring traps, 25
Colony trap, 76-77
Conibear safety gripper, 42
Conibear traps, 3, 21, 27, 28, 34, 41-42, 81, 96, 108
Conibear trap setter, 41
Coveralls, 56
Coyote, 1, 6, 19, 29, 52, 83-86
Cross fox, 101
Cruelty, 3
Cubbies, 6, 16-17, 19
Cubby sets, 116-117
Culvert set, 79, 115

Deadfalls, 6, 21, 22-23
Deer hair, 19
Depopulation, 15
Dirt hole, 85, 117
Double long-spring, 25, 29, 81
Drags, 110
Droppings, 15
Drowning sets, 4, 118
Dyeing, 33

Eat out, 2
Entrenching tool, 34-36

Ermine, 68
Ethics, 147-148

Fake trap set, 121
Feathers, 19
Firearms, 47-49
Fisher, 17, 52, 104-105
Fleshing, 137-138
Footwear, 55-56
Fox, 1, 16, 19, 29, 52, 99-102
Fox hole shovels, 34-36
Freezing, 61
Fur auction, 140
Furbearer damage, 1

Gambrels, 124
Gloves, 54-55
Gob bait, 19
Gray fox, 99-102
Groundhog, 107-108
Guide stakes, 111

Hatchets, 38
Hip boots, 55
Hog-nosed skunk, 69
Holes, 17
Honemaster, 127
Honey, 50
Hooded skunk, 69
Humane traps, 3, 21, 24, 34

Interval set, 115-116

Jiffy trap setter, 41
Jump traps, 25

Killer-type traps, 3, 21, 27, 28, 34, 41-42, 81, 96, 108
Killing animals, 30
Kleflock snares, 28-29
Kneeling sheet, 38-39

Lanterns, 40-41
Least weasel, 66-67
Leghold traps, 3, 4, 22-23
Lights, 40-41
Live traps, 3, 29-32
Long-tailed weasel, 67-68
Louisiana, 66, 99
Lure, 51-54, 149-153
Lynx, 29, 103-104

Marten, 17, 51, 53, 81-83
Mercaptan, 71
Mink, 6, 16, 17, 30, 51, 53, 77-79, 122
Mink streams, 6, 7, 79

Minnesota, 106
Minnows, 19, 50, 91
Missouri, 6, 20-21, 28, 70, 93
Muskrat floating set, 18, 74, 121
Muskrats, 1, 2, 6, 15, 18, 19, 30, 53, 57,
   72-77, 79, 122

Naphtha, 141, 143
Natural baits, 50-51
Notes, 15, 16
Nutria, 97-99, 122

Obstruction set, 111, 112
Opossum, 6, 16, 17, 53, 63-66
Otter, 79-81, 138

Pan cover, 109
Peak 1 compact lantern, 40-41
Pelts
   Frozen, 124
   Handling, 123-139
   Sales, 139-141
Persimmons, 50
Polecat, 69-70
Preparation of traps, 32-34

Raccoon, 6, 17, 19, 20, 29, 30, 51, 53, 90-93, 124-125
Red fox, 99-102
Resources, renewable, 1
Round stretched pelts, 124
Runs, 15

Salt, 61, 141-142
Scats, 7-15
Scent post, 89, 114
Scents, 51-54
Scouting, 5-16
   Preseason preparation, 16-20
Scrapers, 40, 61
Sets, 109-122
   Baited, 116
   Blind, 110-111
   Bridge, 79-113
   Campfire, 120-121
   Cubby, 116-117
   Culvert, 79, 115
   Drowning, 118
   Fake trap, 121
   Floating, 18, 74, 121
   Hole, 117
   Interval, 115-116
   Obstruction, 111-112
   Rat trap killer, 122
   Scent post, 85, 114
   Shiny object, 119-120
   Spring run, 122
   Trail set, 112
   Water sets, 118
   Wing, 49, 119-120
Shovels, 34-36
Sifter, 36-37
Sign, 7-15
Skinning, 123-129

Skinning gambrel, 124
Skunk, 6, 16, 17, 19, 30, 53, 68-72
Skunk scent, 71-72
Slurry, 15
Smell cat, 70
Snares, 3, 28-29
Spotted skunk, 69
Spring run set, 122
South Dakota, 84
Steel traps, 23-24
Step overs, 111
Stop-loss trap, 26, 76
Stretching equipment, 56-60, 138
Striped skunk, 69
Stripper, 61-62
Supplies, 149-153
Sure-grip trap, 26, 76

Tail stripper, 61-62
Tanning, 141-146
Terrain, 6, 7
Tracks, 8-14
Trail set, 112
Trap setter, 41
Trapper's shorthand, 16
Trapper's tool, 39-40

Waders, 55-56
Wading stick, 38
Washita, 127
Water, 6
Waxing, 33
Weasel, 1, 6, 16, 17, 30, 53, 66-68
   Ermine, 67-68
   Least weasel, 66-67
   Long-tailed, 67-68
Wing set, 49, 119-120
Wire, 36
Wire stretchers, 57, 60, 138
Wolverine, 106-107
Wolves, 106
Wringoff, 76